Red-eared Slider Turtle

Red-eared Slider Turtle Owner's Manual

Red-eared Slider Turtle Pros and Cons, Care,
Housing, Diet and Health.
by

David Donalton

D1524079

Table of Contents

Introduction

The idea of domesticating animals is not new; we have been creating a chain of connections with several species in the animal kingdom for the purpose of peaceful coexistence. History may have taught modern man to breed cattle, horses and poultry for personal consumption and profit; our relationship with animals today, however, has become more complex, even emotional.

We now view animals, not only as a source of profit, but also as a source of love and companionship. Through our discovery of new species and their natures, we have also modified the concept of domestication, with exotic animals being domesticated with as much enthusiasm - and considerable success - as the conventional ones. What is fascinating, however, is that people tend to have varied preferences when asked to select an animal they would like for companionship.

For some, the perfect animal companion is one that is energetic, affectionate and boisterous. Those with a quiet demeanour may prefer an animal that is well-behaved, disciplined and calm. Some may describe their perfect companions to be those who swim behind large glass enclosures, providing tranquillity and beauty. And some others still may choose to bring home those pets that can be trained and raised for long-term profits. If you belong to that elite group of people who seek a pet that does not require constant handling and attention, is at least partly aquatic by nature but can be contained within an enclosure, a red-eared slider turtle may be the right choice for you.

Of the over 300 species of turtles and tortoises that are found around the world, only a handful have been observed to be suitable for captivity and domestication. The limit posed by Wildlife and Game laws and the aversion towards domestication displayed by many chelonian breeds makes it additionally challenging to house and rear just about any breed of turtle-whether aquatic or terrestrial - available. After a prolonged history of exposure to humans, however, the Red-eared Slider turtle – found primarily in the North American continent has today emerged as the most popular breed of turtles requested as pets. Its increasing popularity as a pleasing pet, along with its positive depiction in the media has further made it available in South and Central America, Europe, Bahrain and even across the Australian continent.

Cold-blooded and water-loving by nature, these diurnal members of the reptile family prefer to spend their existence larger underwater, while emerging above to engage in basking, foraging and egg-laying behaviors, with some hours of the day devoted towards rest. Despite their curious natures, red-eared slider turtles, like other pond-slider turtle breeds, display an aversion towards being handled unless absolutely necessary, and will respond by hissing, scratching, kicking, biting or withdrawing into their shell.

A quality that makes the red-eared slider turtle a prized pet is its ability to live for up to 30 or more years, if given proper care and attention. Provided it is housed in a safe enclosure that closely regulates temperature, lighting and heat settings, receives plenty of food for immediate feeding and protection from predators and infections, your red-eared slider will provide you with lifelong companionship, while becoming a pleasing, quiet and graceful part of your home environment.

These omnivorous creatures have healthy appetites, but require relatively less feed per day when compared to other animals intended for domestication, such as dogs. They are also prone to bursts of aggression and hostility during the breeding season, and may become aggressive towards each other in order to secure a mate or protect the eggs from the rest of the flock. On the flip side, those red-eared sliders who are relatively comfortable around humans can also make for relatively sociable companions that will pick a treat or two from the hands of those caregivers they trust.

This family of chelonians are also of relatively robust health, rarely succumbing to the communicable, life-threatening illnesses that plague other domesticated breeds such as cattle or poultry. Common health-related ailments may include superficial wounds and injuries sustained to the shell or limbs during fights, infections contracted due to inhospitable and unhygienic housing conditions, or as a result of a nutritional deficiency through an improper diet.

The health and well-being of red-eared slider turtles in captivity is largely reliant on the kind of living environment you can provide; these pond-sliders will require rigorous conditions to meet in terms of housing, feeding and healthcare. In favorable and nurturing environments, red-eared sliders can also be extremely easy to breed, whether for personal use or for profit.

What does place the ownership of red-eared slider turtles in slightly tricky territory is their status around the world as one of the top 100 invasive species in the natural ecosystem. Displaying a variety of innate survival advantages over other turtle, reptile and animal breeds in a similar space, red-eared sliders can easily out-compete existing species, and then over-populate any environment they inhabit (whether in the wild or in captivity).

Their additional status as carriers of salmonella, coupled with the considerable cost needed to maintain them may make their ownership and possession slightly more legally and socially complicated that several other domesticated animals. It is no wonder, then, that red-eared slider turtles are enthusiastically given a home usually by caregivers on two extremes of the ownership scale – either those who have little understanding of the things that are involved to care for this pet, or those who have a complete awareness of these terrapins and their need to be given long-term captive housing.

If you, too, wish to bring home red-eared slider turtles, through this book, you will gain deeper insight into its world - from its natural settings, to its behavioral patterns. You will also be guided through every stage of owning these pond-sliding, quirky terrapins, from initial thought to long-term care for personal companionship. With a positive attitude and a dedicated spirit, you can work past the challenges that come with housing red-eared slider turtles, and make them an enriching part of your life.

Chapter 1: Meet the Red-eared Slider Turtle

The Trachemys Scripta Elegans, or Red-eared Slider Turtle, is one of about 19 species of pond-slider turtles found around the world, and the most common among the 3 pond-slider species found in the United States of America. Poikilothermic by nature, these diurnal reptiles belonging to the family of chelonians (comprising of all tortoises and turtles) share such their natural habitat and many behavioral traits with its American slider counterparts, the yellow-bellied and Cumberland slider turtles.

It is the distinctive wide stripe in a vibrant hue of red found near the turtle's ear, along with its ability to "slide" off surfaces into the water that contribute towards its name. With a preference for freshwater aquatic spaces surrounding by soft, muddy banks in slightly warmer and regulated temperatures, the medium-sized, omnivorous red-eared slider turtles have been found to comfortably inhabit a large number of eco spaces, making them a popular choice among exotic pet enthusiasts.

1. The Relationship between Red-eared Slider Turtles and Humans

With small, elongated shell-encased bodies and a pleasing and attractively marked face, – it is not hard to see why humans would take an instant liking to red-eared slider turtles – or any of a variety of other semi-aquatic and land-dwelling chelonians, for that matter. While the relationship between turtles and humans dates back enough centuries to warrant their presence in local and traditional culinary and medicinal use as well as folklore, it is the red-eared terrapin that brought the pond-sliding family of turtles into the spotlight as a domestic pet in the 1900s.

First spotted in the Mississippi river valley in the United States, the abundance of red-eared sliders in the wild, coupled with their relatively non-threatening nature and small-size led to these pets being taken in from the wild as pets. This trend caught on so quickly and effectively, that up to 10 million red-eared slider turtles were believed to have been exported before 1960, both within and outside the North American continent. Their popularity as attractive aquatic pets sold at very low prices also made them a staple at several county fairs, also earning them the nickname "dime-store turtles".

As is inevitable with the domestication of any previously untamed breed, the first owners, breeders and farmers of red-eared slider turtles as pets had little knowledge and resources to provide the proper sanitary care needed to house cold-blooded reptiles. An inadequate awareness of the chelonians feeding habits, behavioral patterns and health requirement led to thousands of red-eared sliders being fed such unfit food as offal from slaughterhouses, before their sale. It comes as no surprise, then, that such unnatural caring rituals resulted in the chelonians becoming carriers – and transmitters – of such lethal parasites as salmonella and bacteria Arizona.

After thousands of salmonella-related deaths among children and red-eared slider farmers by 1960, the 4-inch law was eventually passed in 1975, prohibiting the sale of those turtles with a shell-length of under 4 inches (100 mm).

One of the most popular pets worldwide, red-eared slider turtles now found themselves rejected as companions in captivity. To adhere with the law, many chelonians found themselves abruptly released into the wild, forcing them to adapt to unfamiliar habitats and new ecosystems. It is thanks to the survival ability of this chelonian that the red-eared slider turtle managed to out-compete and outlast most native species in its new housing spaces, becoming a common fixture across a range of non-native environments.

Residents, red-eared slider farmers and the governments of these non-native habitats (the rest of the North American continent, Europe, Australia) were now overwhelmed with a growing red-eared terrapin population and inadequate resources to care for them in the wild. First classifying the breed as an invasive species, several advancements were made to help prevent the spread of salmonella through vaccinations, sanitary housing, and proper food and health care. Owners and breeders, on the other hand, were given better training and education on how to properly care for exotic pets such as red-eared sliders.

It is around this time that the syndication of the popular children's cartoon "Teenage Mutant Ninja Turtles" came to everyone's rescue. Gaining widespread fame among adults and children for their quirky personalities and heroic archetypes, the fictional turtles were revealed to be red-eared slider turtles in an early episode of the show. They, thus, single handed managed to bring about a resurgence in the sale of red-eared sliders in the United States and especially in Britain.

In today's times, the tumultuous relationship between red-eared slider turtles and human beings hangs on a precarious balance determined by the right kind of care, housing and healthcare provided to the turtles. While the European Union and Australia has outlawed the import of red eared sliders owing to their negative impacts on the ecology, many other countries and states in the United States still allow the sale and domestication of these reptiles, though under strict conditions.

This resurgence in sales coupled with a better knowledge on the care provided to reptiles in captivity has also proved to be useful to those farmers who ship red-eared sliders to south-east Asian countries for culinary, medicinal and religious purposes.

The link between salmonella, ecosystem invasion, pet turtle trade and the 4-inch law

When we mention the purchase of red-eared slider turtles for domestication in the United States of America, a discussion on the 4-inch law, its history, need and contemporary relevance is inevitable. A law put into place by the United Stated Food and Drug Administration in 1975, the 4-inch remains a controversial and highly debated subject among naturists, chelonian breeds and individual owners.

To explain the 4-inch law in a nutshell, the sale of red-eared slider turtles with a carapace-length of under 4 inches (100 mm) is prohibited across the United States. This law was considered necessary after the overwhelming sale of this terrapin from the 1900s to the 1960s, coupled with insufficient knowledge on the care of the reptile, led to a deadly spread of salmonella among citizens, particularly children. It was determined that the younger red-eared hatchlings with their smaller shell-length could easily fit into children's mouths, giving the children salmonella through casual contact.

A better awareness in today's times on the raising of these turtles, on the other hand, has led to sharp decline in cases related to salmonella contraction from red-eared sliders. Better healthcare, housing facilities and an awareness of the right hygiene while handling the chelonians has raised several questions on the contemporary relevance of this law. Younger and smaller red-eared sliders are no more of a salmonella hazard than their adult counterparts, and both groups can be successfully housed provided basic cleanliness rituals are followed.

Interestingly, while it may have been salmonella that caused the 4-inch law to come into effect, territories across the United States have been more severely affected by invasiveness of these terrapins in their ecosystems. With the increasing early desire to own these popular pets coupled with an inadequate knowledge on the care of red-eared sliders, several red-eared slider turtles, or their hatchlings were released into the wild by early owners. When transported across the United States, Europe and Australia, it is this invasive nature that demanded the eventual need for laws on the ownership of this reptile.

2. Natural Range and Habitat

The ability to adapt with ease to the semi-aquatic eco space to which they are introduced is probably why red-eared slider turtles have gained inclusion into that selective club of invasive species. This resilience to embrace and virtually overtake a set of climatic conditions, food and terrains has helped this terrapin thrive, both the Northern as well as the Southern Hemispheres.

In the Americas, you're most likely to find red-eared sliders in abundance from the state of Illinois within the Mississippi Valley all the way down to Mexico, including such states as Arizona, Massachusetts, California, Kentucky, Pennsylvania, Ohio, Texas, Michigan, West Virginia, Hawaii and Alabama. The Central and South American countries of Mexico, Brazil, Uruguay and Venezuela also now house a healthy red-eared slider population.

Across the ocean, red-eared slider turtles, though not native to this geography, continue to comfortably inhabit the vast expanse of the Eurasian region. Owing mostly to the practice of introducing these turtles into a new ecosystem in captivity, and then releasing them into the wild with upon dissatisfaction or by accident, expect to see lots of red-eared sliders in the United Kingdom, Italy, France and Germany. As we move eastwards, red-eared sliders once again become abundant in East Asia, in Japan, South Korea, Thailand, Guam and Israel.

Red-eared sliders have also shown a fondness for the mildly tropical climates of the African region, with a particular liking for South Africa and Egypt. And further still, red-eared slider turtles have made their homes in the southern regions of Australia and New Zealand, through introduction to the continent by early human visitors.

It seems fairly clear by now that red-eared slider turtles will find a way to adapt to nearly any location, provided it consists of a thriving freshwater system with soft and wet surrounding land areas. Even though this member of the semi-aquatic basking family inhabits a wide variety of spaces, it is the quiet, swampy lands with privacy to forage, mate and build nesting zones that they show the highest preference for. Many breeds of sliders, particular the read-eared ones, are perfectly content as a basking species that occupy the banks of rivers, ponds, streams, lakes and swamps. For its part, the terrestrial part of their habitat is considered adequate so long as it comprises undisturbed spots for basking and burrowing.

Perhaps the only prerequisite that red-eared slider turtles look for before settling in is the depth of the surrounding water body. Their preferred settlements mostly comprise of waters that measure over a metre in depth, in order to facilitate swimming and underwater foraging for plant life. Aside from this one determining factor, as long as a location contains a sustainable food source, a water body and some level of privacy, you can expect a community of red-eared slider turtles housed comfortably until the time depleted water levels force them to migrate.

3. Red-eared Slider Turtles and the Ecology

Red-eared slider turtles have managed to carve a unique and complicated existential zone within the ecology, thanks to their choice of habitat, behavioural patterns and feeding habits. Within the vast ecological space, red-eared sliders find themselves categorized with their medium-sized counterparts that live in semi-aquatic conditions. In addition, red-eared slider turtles further slot themselves into a niche by being pond-sliding, land-nesting reptiles of medium-size who are also omnivorous in nature. Within these parameters, however, red-eared slider turtles have found themselves contributing in ways that may seem detrimental to their non-native ecosystems.

As is the law of nature, red-eared sliders, like all other living beings, play certain direct and indirect roles to help maintain ecological balance in their native space. Through such activities as foraging and breeding, these turtles not only take an active part in population control of several plant and animal species, but also contribute towards the growth of their own. Their vulnerability as eggs or hatchlings, along with their brumative state in the winter makes these medium-sized chelonians desired foods for larger animals like raccoons, foxes, birds of prey and other carnivorous turtles.

What complicates this terrapin's relationship with the ecology, however, is its existence and subsequent thriving in non-native habitats. Transported outside their native Mississippi river valley habitat owing to growing popularity, red-eared slider turtles became a significant part of other terrains in the North-American continent, then crossing over to Europe and Australia. A variety of factors, such as the growing rate of salmonella-related deaths, inadequate resources to care for terrapins in captivity and unsanitary breeding and farming practices led to the prohibition of these terrapins as pets by 1975.

Now released into the wild, other native slider turtle species, along with the local flora and fauna soon discovered the red-eared slider turtle's superiority in any given ecosystem. Capable of breeding with yellow-bellied slider turtles, red-eared sliders released in these areas were found to be the dominant provider of genes, thereby corrupting the local breed's gene pool. As cold-blooded reptiles with the need to bask, red-eared sliders were found to successfully occupy prominent basking zones, preventing other breeds from accessing essential sunlight and warmth.

These hardy creatures were also found to be adept at foraging for food, while capable of surviving cold winter conditions by entering a state of brumation.

To add to the growing list of ways by which red-eared sliders prove to be successful competitors in non-native territories, it is this species of pond-slider that is believed to bring salmonella and other infections to those areas where it thrives. As a result, this subspecies of chelonian may not enjoy favour with several Wildlife authorities – a fact clearly emphasized by its inclusion on the list of invasive species.

We know today, that proper care, sanitation practices and a controlled environment can help red-eared slider turtle thrive in captivity, and prevent them from spreading infectious illnesses.

Their negative impact in non-native environments, however, has been so significant, that several governments make the choice to eradicate its population, rather than preserve it.

It is perhaps this indifferent nature towards red-eared slider turtles, therefore, that makes its care in captivity essential. In a hygienic environment that can guarantee no competition with other species for food, light and heat, red-eared slider turtles can generate arguments towards the invasive tag attached to them. Provided the necessary provision are made in areas of long-term population control and health care, it can be ensured that red-eared slider turtles not contribute negatively towards the ecosystem in which they exist.

Chapter 2: Understand your Red-eared Slider Turtle

1. Physical Traits and Appearance

An adult red-eared slider turtle is a medium-sized member of the pond-slider family, usually growing to a shell length between inches (mm), settling in at a weight in the range of 100 and 200gms, reaching even 300gms in weight in captive conditions. A healthy adult red-eared slider is often classified by the above optimum shell length and weight, along with four other important characteristic physical traits:

1) A wide stripe behind the eye area in hues of red,

2) A distinct V-shaped notch along the rounded underside of its chin,

3) A smoothly-textured oval-shaped dark green shell carapace (top part of the shell),

4) And prominent yellow and green stripes visible across the carapace, face and legs.

The adult red-eared terrapins skin is often olive to greenish in color, with a brightly green-colored carapace that darkens with age. It is the markings around the face, carapace and plastron (lower part of the shell) that differentiate the red-eared sliders from other North American varieties. The plastron is bright yellow in color and will have visible dark markings across its surface. On the surface of the carapace, you will find pronounced scaled-divisions, known as scutes. Developed through calcium intake, these scutes from the external covering for the shell will shed and regrow on a regular basis. The shell itself is smooth to touch, oval and elongated in shape and possess a distinct keel or bend in the centre to aid swimming and digging activities.

The limbs of a red-eared slider turtle are strong, thick and extend in clawed digits with webbed undersides, designed for agile swimming, adept digging and unique mating rituals.

Adult male red-eared slider turtles have been studied to grow to a size comparably smaller to their female counterparts. With an average shell-size of 5 to 8 inches, adult male red-eared terrapins are also told apart from females through such markers as longer, more curved claws used for mating, a longer and prominently thicker tail and the farther position of their cloaca from the carapace than female red-eared sliders.

Red-eared slider turtles have an average life expectancy of around 20 to 30, even 50 years in the wild, sometimes living for a shorter period in captivity. As part of this considerably long lifespan, red-eared slider turtles develop at their own pace, reaching full maturation and adulthood between the ages of 2 and 7 years, depending on the gender and size of the shell.

Sex determination and the red-eared slider turtle

While there may be certain characteristic features that differentiate adult male red-eared slider turtles from the females, these distinctions are only prominent once the turtles have attained sexual maturity. Unlike several other animals, red-eared sliders possess an anatomy whose gender-distinct sexual maturity is governed by the dimensions of its shell in the males, and its age in years in the females.

Almost identical in appearance at birth, male red-eared slider turtles only develop distinct tail and claw sizes once they have attained a shell length of 90 to 100 mm (4 inches). This achievement in physical structure is reached between the ages of 2 and 5 years, depending on the individual terrapin.

Among the female red-eared slider turtles, on the other hand, the optimum shell length for sexual maturity ranging between 160 to 200 mm (6-7.5 in) could be attained much before they are physically ready to engage in courtship, mating, nesting and egg-laying behaviours. Female red-eared slider turtles have been found to attain sexual maturity between the ages of 5 to 7 years, with a large shell-size directly hinting at a larger egg clutch-carrying capacity.

It is not just the attainment of sexual maturity that is unique to red-eared slider turtles, but also the phenomenon through which their sex is determined at the incubation stage. Regardless of the dominance of chromosomes at the time of embryonic development, the sex of the red-eared slider turtle is determined by the ambient temperature of its incubation setting.

While male red-eared sliders are guaranteed to be born in temperatures ranging between 23 and 29 degrees Celsius, female red-eared slider turtles can be hatched by incubating the eggs in temperature of 29 to 31 degrees Celsius. To further add to the uniqueness of the sex determining phenomenon, incubating the eggs at the median temperature can also successfully breed transgender hatchlings – resulting in a high success rate with breeding endeavors in a controlled environment.

2. Different Types of Slider Turtles:

Red-Eared Slider Turtle

- Official name: Trachemys Scripta Elegans
- Natural Range: Mississippi valley (Mississippi, Illinois, Missouri, Kansas, Ohio, Oklahoma, Arkansas, Texas, Kentucky, Tennessee, Louisiana, West Virginia), Australia, Asia, Europe
- Adult Size (Shell diameter):
    - Male: 3-5 in (90-125 mm)
    - Female: 6-11 in (150-300 mm)
- Appearance:
    - Body:
        - Colour: Olive Green
        - Markings: Reddish wide stripe behind eyes
    - Shell:
        - Colour: Dark green carapace, yellow pastron
        - Markings: Yellow stripes on carapace, black markings on pastron
        - Shape: Oval and smooth
- Life expectancy (years):
    - Wild: 20-30
    - Captive: 30-50

Cumberland Slider Turtle

- Official name: Trachemys Scripta Troostii
- Natural range: United States: Cumberland river valley (Kentucky and Tennessee), Mississippi, Georgia and Alabama
- Adult Size (shell diameter):
    - Male: 6 in (154mm)
    - Female: 11 in (279 mm)
- Appearance:
    - Body:
        - Colour: Olive Green

- Markings: yellow patches on the neck, legs, "S" shaped stripe on face
  - o Shell
    - Colour: Brown/black carapace, yellow pastron
    - Markings: Yellow stripes on carapace, black markings on pastron
    - Shape: Oval.
- Life expectancy (years):
  - Wild: 20-30
  - Captive: 40-60

Yellow-Bellied Slider Turtle

- Official name: Trachemys Scripta
- Natural range: United States: South-eastern plains and coastal states (Alabama, Virginia, Georgia, North and South Carolina, Florida).Mexico, Brazil, Venezuela, Argentina, Uruguay, Canada, China, Japan, France, Italy
- Adult Size (shell diameter):
  - Male: 5-9 in (130-230 mm)
  - Female: 18-13 in (200-330 mm)
- Appearance:
  - o Body:
    - Colour: Olive green
    - Markings: yellow patches on the neck, legs, "S" shaped stripe on face
  - o Shell
    - Colour: Brown/ black carapace, yellow pastron
    - Markings: yellow stripes on carapace, black markings on plastron
    - Shape: Oval
- Life expectancy (years):
  - Wild: 20-30
  - Captive: 40-60

3. Red-eared Slider Turtles and the Reproductive cycle

Between the months of March and July, come breeding season, the female red-eared slider turtle will choose one from two or more simultaneous suitors to engage in a mating ritual and fertilize her eggs. This selected male will often display the most unique of the courtship dances, and may also be the most aggressive of the flock. It is often such expressive behavior that makes a red-eared slider male attractive to sexually active females.

The act of courtship is undertaken when a sexually viable male posits himself in the path of female turtle underwater, extends his front limbs and uses his claws to create repeated vibrations on the head and neck areas of the female's body. This feat is achieved with the male occasionally biting the female behind the neck, and with both sexes swimming in opposite directions: the female, swimming forward and the male, in the opposite direction.

The act of mating itself is carried out when an aroused and receptive female will cease swimming and allow herself to gently sink to the floor. The male then mounts the female upon receiving her attention, and grabs her firmly with his limbs around her carapace, and tucks his tail in firmly under hers. The male attempts to create cloacal contact by swimming backwards while releasing his front limbs, placing him in an upright posture - an act that may appear aggressive and hostile, but in fact, is pleasurable to the female.

The mating ritual will generally last for up to 15 minutes with insemination culminating the act. The female red-eared slider then spends the time between May and June modifying her diet to sustain her eggs and digging up a nest to lay her first clutch of the season in. As the female red-eared slider possess the ability to hold the male's sperm within her and keep it viable for up to a year; this allows several females the opportunity to conduct mating rituals well before the breeding season begins, in order to gain a quick start on nesting and hatching.

The nesting period brings out the most aggressive behaviour among female red-eared slider turtles in the wild; many females, especially those engaged in digging, burrowing and egg-depositing, tend to become aggressive not only towards other animals, but also towards their mates.

Domesticated red-eared slider turtle females, if provided with the right setting, will replicate the art of nest-building in the wild by digging up soft soil with her hind limbs in a deep spot available in their premises. Amniotes by nature, red-eared terrapins, despite their fondness for the water, will create their nesting zone on land, which is chosen to be not more than 200 metres away from an abundant freshwater source.

Usually ready by the latter hours of the afternoon, the resulting hole will often measure between 3 and 10 inches in diameter and 2 to 4 inches in depth. Into this hole, the female will deposit between 2 and 25 eggs, with a white shell and leathery surface. Upon reaching her desired number to complete the clutch, the female then covers up the nest with the moist soil covering, camouflaging the site by neatly packing in the mud.

Several studies have shown a direct relationship between the size of the female red-eared terrapin plastron and the resulting size of the clutch; it can be safely argued that larger-sized females tend to deposit larger-sized clutches than their smaller counterparts. Depending on how early she accomplishes the insemination, nesting and oviposition of the eggs, a female red-eared terrapin could lay between 3 and 5 clutches in a single breeding season. It is seldom that the succeeding egg clutches are oviposited in the same spot as the first clutch; laying red-eared slider mothers prefer to scatter their eggs among various safe nesting sites.

Red-eared slider eggs only begin the process of development and hatching when they receive the first bout of incubation after oviposition; it is for this reason that the nesting site is chosen with great care to contain optimum direct sunlight, warmth, water and food sources.

Provided the female red-eared slider safely incubate her eggs for an extended period, hatchlings will emerge from the eggs after about 60 to 75, even 80 days – in the days between July and September. The hatchling first emerges by forming a tiny hole or "pip" in the shell. Chipping away at the eggshell with an especially formed calcified tip, hatchlings will successfully break out of their shell after a few hours from the first crack. Curiously, those hatchlings that were oviposited at the end of the breeding season towards the fall months may also choose to brumate and incubate during winter, breaking out only at the first sign of spring.

While little in size at about 25 mm at the time of hatching, the late blooming hatchlings – also called juveniles – emerge from their brumative state measuring an inch in length. Ready for the external world and requiring – and receiving – little or no parental care, most young ones make a speedy growth towards the two-inch mark by the end of the first year. For the first few months, young hatchlings subsist largely on carnivorous feed for sustenance, incorporating more herbivorous elements in their food after the first year. It is with age that the bright green hue of the carapace darkens and physical growth slows down, until the male and female turtles each reach the suitable shell lengths – between 200-250 mm in males and 250-300 mm in females that signals sexual maturity.

4. Common behavioural patterns

Red-eared slider turtles, depending on the time of year and their level of interaction with other animals, possess a varied range of behavioral patterns that make them interesting to observe, both in the wild and in captivity. Common to all pond-dwelling basking turtles, however, red-eared sliders are linked to each other through such common behaviors as basking, nesting, brumating, and displaying unique mating rituals coupled with aggressive behavior.

Red-eared slider turtles, while being largely hostile towards other species and humans, show fairly sociable natures that encourage interaction with other pond-sliders. Preferring to rest alone at night, but bask together during the day, adult red-eared sliders share such duties as feeding, basking and mating, while sparing no attention towards caring for the young. While some red-eared slider settlements may be small in size, their love for basking at optimal spots in their natural setting means that you can easily spot a group of over 5 or 10 red-eared terrapins basking while stacked atop each other near pond or lake clearings.

Basking in particular, seems to be a preferred behavioral trait among several all pond-sliding species, let alone the red-eared slider - not only has this practice found to be healthy for the upkeep of the reptile's shell and body temperature, but has also been observed to provide a deep sense of pleasure to the chelonians themselves. So great is the pleasure derived during basking rituals, that other smaller animals or varieties of pond-sliding turtles, such as the yellow-bellied slider, may often be aggressively chased away from prized basking zones.

Not particularly known for their sensory abilities, red-eared sliders are believed to possess poor hearing, making up for this deficit with sharper responses to vibration in the environment. This ability to sense vibrations helps them stay alert even while basking or napping underwater. With no designated space reserved for sleep and rest during the darker hours of the day, red-eared slider turtles spend their sleeping hours floating gently across the water, usually in secluded and hidden areas with plenty of protective yet soft cover.

Another common behavior pattern shared by species of pond-sliding family is the tendency to "slide" from their terrestrial basking spots into the water without any other seeming movement. It is, in fact, this sliding motion that lends this group of terrapins its name. Owing to their small size compared to larger animals in the ecosystem, red-eared slider turtles will rarely attempt to confront their predators or sources of threat, choosing instead to evade capture by abruptly sliding into the water or retreating into their shell. While a successful means of evasion in the wild, this startled reaction in a captive setting often proves stressful to the terrapin's health.

Chapter 3: The Red-eared Slider Turtle as a Pet

1. Red-eared Slider Turtles are a Lifelong commitment

Their striking appearance, content demeanour while swimming and basking, and pleasing, almost smirking visage may deceive many aspiring caregivers into believing that red-eared slider turtles require little space and attention in order to thrive. These chelonians, however, have been classified as exotic pets with good reason. An exotic animal is so labelled when it demands specific care, housing and handling techniques for its optimum survival – red-eared slider turtles fulfil these requisites by requiring voluminous tanks to swim, bask, feed and burrow in, a varied diet to maintain their health, and deliberate behavioral and medical treatment.

By nature, red-eared slider turtles are known to be curious and aggressive, with a penchant for wandering about the premises in search of food and water. This inquisitive nature, however, should not be mistaken for friendliness; many terrapins may take weeks, even months to domesticate. Until you can forge a relationship of trust with your pet, the red-eared slider turtle will resist any attempts at being touched, held or grabbed. With independent personalities and reptilian thought processes, red-eared sliders may also never entirely become comfortable around your presence, and may have to be left undisturbed.

Despite their independent natures, however, red-eared slider turtles can also be very needy once they bond with their caregivers and identify them as primary sources of food. In the wild, these terrapins rely on available resources in natures for nutrition and shelter. With timely feeding habits, and a tendency to beg for food that is dense in protein, it becomes the caregiver's responsibility to ensure that the dietary needs of their pets are met, as well as regulated. Care also needs to be taken on behalf of the red-eared slider to ensure that all elements in the housing zone are compatible with the turtle's health and safety.

Apart from providing conditions that promote physical wellbeing, red-eared slider turtles also require daily periods engaging in basking and swimming in order to thrive, with special provisions made for their comfort during the winter months. Periods of extended neglect towards such responsibilities as regular filtration of water, or cleaning away of food and excrement particles may make your terrapin mortally ill, or may cause it distress.

Red-eared slider turtles are also diurnal in nature, and are active for about 17 hours of the day. In order to successfully forge a bond with your chipmunks, you will have to ensure that your daily schedules coincide with the waking hours of your pet, while still providing them with the privacy they may demand during basking or feeding; should you work during the day, it may be best consider nocturnal pets such as Tiger Salamanders.

If the exacting care standards required by these chelonians cannot be met, it is best to re-think your decision to house red-eared slider turtles, whether for companionship or subsequent profit. On the other hand, if you sustain a lifestyle that can comfortably incorporate a pet as demanding yet detached as the red-eared slider turtle, you may find that they make for entertaining, amusing and rewarding lifelong pets.

2. Are Red-eared Slider Turtles kid-friendly pets?

It is probably due to their deceptively pleasing appearance, along with their depiction in the media as lovable cartoon or wise storybook characters, that red-eared slider turtles are believed to be suitable pets for people of all ages. If you are bringing a red-eared terrapin to a house that has children, or plan to gift one to a young child, however, you should take the time to consider that this may not be the wisest idea.

While it is definitely not true for all children, most younger caregivers and red-eared slider turtles may not always form a friendly and nurturing bond. This unlikelihood can largely be attributed to the aggressive and often distant personalities of the average red-eared slider, and the easiness with which children can become bored of carrying out ritualistic responsibilities.

We have already discussed how these chelonians, as exotics, require a specific method of caregiving that addresses their food, health, habitat and emotional needs. The child will also need to put in the requisite bonding time needed to tame the terrapin and make it comfortable around its presence. Since the process of familiarising oneself with a reptile can take days, even weeks to accomplish, a child may quickly become impatient, when an adult would understand the time needed to do the same.

Due to their aversion at being held or handled - at least initially - children may find themselves being regularly nipped or scratched at when they try to grab their chelonian pets. Many children may additionally be repulsed by slippery feel of a turtles body. Again, a reasonable adult, or even child, should know that these reptiles only bite as an act of defence, but many children tend to process the attack as an act of open hostility. This may lead to the child either abandon the pet for fear of being bitten again, or may trigger the child's anger and cause them to hurt the pet by way of payback.

If your pet turtle is relatively tame and can socialize comfortably with children, it becomes your responsibility to ensure that the terrapin is handled the right way. With slithery skin and a wriggly nature, red-eared sliders can be easily dropped if held without proper care. Furthermore, while a child may want to squeeze the pet in their palms as a sign of affection, they may not realize the consequence of their actions. If left unattended in a tank with no covering, red-eared sliders will gladly climb out of their housing spaces, getting lost as a result of prolonged wandering or becoming an easy target for larger predators.

Red-eared slider turtles are not the type of domestic pet that can be handled without extreme caution exercised on the owner's part. With a disposition towards carrying and spreading salmonella at any point in their lives, daily handling of a red-eared slider turtle requires rigorous washing and disinfecting of hands, clothes and items that come into contact with the pets. Any missed opportunity at cleaning up may potentially expose your children to a salmonella infection at worst. With their infamous status as an invasive ecological species, should your child find themselves dissatisfied with their pet, several local laws will prevent you from setting it back into the wild – making the pet your lifelong responsibility.

It is not just young children, but also teenagers who are generally advised against housing red-eared slider turtles, if they cannot provide the exacting care the exotics need. A spacious housing facility with provisions for a terrestrial as well as aquatic setting, a steady routine that complements the chelonians lifestyle and a stable income are prerequisites for acquiring a red-eared slider turtle as a pet - factors that children, teenagers, students and unemployed or lower-income group members are often unable to fulfil. If the terrapin is housed in such cramped spaces as dormitory rooms or bathroom shelves, and is left neglected during its feeding and cleaning periods, it can become easily stressed, develop behavioural disorders, fall ill or even drown.

This does not mean that children and teenagers are to be completely banned from raising or handling red-eared slider turtles. It is simply important that you, as a responsible caregiver, educate younger members on the right ways to interact with and care for these pets before you consider bringing them home. Awareness of the difference between an exotic and a common household pet such as dog or cat, can go a long way in preparing younger children to live with the challenging, but fascinating red-eared slider turtle.

3. Initial investments and continued costs

It is often wrongly assumed that a small, semi-aquatic pet such as a Red-eared slider will not require too much money to either bring home or raise. In truth, any exotic, let alone a turtle, can make a considerable dent in your monthly savings, by way of upkeep and maintenance. Your pet will require specific living conditions, food and medical attention to thrive; in addition, the longevity of their lifespan demands that you provide these exacting conditions for approximately 30 years at least. This makes it essential for you to consider whether you can afford its care.

As a potential caregiver, you will first need to invest approximately USD 400 to 700 (around 265 to 465 British pounds) to create a set-up for your red-eared slider. Depending on the number of turtles you plan to bring home, an average-sized tank with a 75-gallon capacity and no extra attachments will cost you between 150 and 450 USD (100-300 British pounds).

This price excludes the inner essential elements that make up an ideal environment for your pet. You will have to provide tank furnishings and flooring elements, such as water filters and heaters, UVA and UVB lighting fixtures, lamp reflectors and thermometers. For their basking needs, your housing should also include a basking platform along with heat lamps as a backup basking measure.

Other elements in the tank will include materials that make up the substrate, aquatic plants, water testing and treatment kits, etc. This phase of preparing the habitat should set you back by an additional 150 to 300 USD (100-200 British pounds), but can also amount to a larger sum, depending on the number of elements and quality of components you add to the tank.

The next financial considerations should be made towards the food you provide your pets with. Your red-eared sliders, especially if brought home as hatchlings, will need a steady diet of nutritious food, in the form of protein, pellets and mineral supplements. As they settle into a routine with you, you can monitor their feeding habits and adjust their feed based on their individual habits. To start, apart from prepared commercial feeds at 10 USD (6 British pound) per can, stocking up on food for your grown pets will cost you at least 40 USD (25 British pounds) a month for fruits and vegetables, with live feed and supplements adding another 30 to 40 USD (20-25 British pounds) to your budget. This cost will likely fluctuate based on the food preferences and growth of your red-eared sliders.

None of the above expenses even begin to cover the healthcare your red-eared sliders will require, from the cursory starter visit to the exotic pet expert and vaccinations, which are estimated to cost between 80 and 120 USD (50-80 British pounds). Regular monthly check-ups can run an annual bill ranging between 20 and 100 USD (15-60 British pounds), and a probable surgical procedure or laboratory test will cost an addition 100 to 200 USD (60-140 British pounds). It is only once these primary arrangements are made can you consider the actual cost of a pet red-eared slider turtle.

The average cost of purchasing this popular terrapin ranges from 10 USD (6 British pounds) for adult red-eared sliders to upwards of 50 USD (30 British pounds), depending on the source your pet is acquired from, and the genetics of the turtle itself. Private breeders and fanciers are known for raising tamer and healthier turtles than their store-bought counterparts – but they also cost more than the latter.

Many pet red-eared sliders are sold by breeders and fanciers who offer to ship the pets to locations that allow the ownership of these exotics. Since the United States is the most popular source for reputed red-eared slider breeders, your shipping fees, depending on your location and that of your seller, may add anything from 30 USD to 75 USD (20-50 British pounds) to your initial investment.

For a healthy quality of life that is neither too sparse nor too excessive for the turtles, you should be prepared to part with about 700-1500 USD (450-1000 British pounds) as an initial investment for a pair of red-eared slider turtles, and then budget around 150 to 200 USD (65-140 British pounds) every month for habitat upkeep, activities such as basking and brumating, food and healthcare.

4. Legal Considerations
For those who like the unique and possibly detached perspective on domestication that Red-eared slider turtles have to offer, the chelonians make for easy-to-please, laidback companions. If you

have already decided that this terrapin is your pet of choice, you may also take a special interest in the process through which your red-eared slider reaches you. Vast though their natural range may be, not all red-eared slider turtles are up for picking and housing at the individual's will.

The invasive nature of several subspecies of the slider turtle family, accompanied by their status as carriers of salmonella means that they receive special regulation across the North American, Australian and European continents. While some of these rules lay certain restrictions on the purchase and possession of these chelonians, other laws may prohibit the acquisition or probable release into the wild of any red-eared sliders altogether. Therefore, in order to protect yourself, is it essential that you have some clarity on the legality behind buying and owning a red-eared slider turtle.

It wouldn't be surprising if you had your heart set on owning a red-eared slider turtle. You must know, however, that selling, buying, possessing and releasing any of these chelonians is illegal in Florida and Oregon, and is governed by strict regulations in several other states whose local plant and animal life have been negatively impacted by its population. If you live in Washington, it helps to know that it is only a group of lobbyists who have been able to temporarily thwart the decision to outlaw these terrapins from the state altogether.

If you do live in a North American state that permits you to house a red-eared slider turtle, you may find yourself turning to the legal pages once again, should you make certain decisions regarding your pet's development. Certain activities, such as the breeding, sale of eggs or hatchlings, or even releasing a captive terrapin into the wild can be met with severe penalties – either a fine, imprisonment, or both.

Furthermore, the extent of invasiveness of this species in such non-native areas as Europe and Australia have forced them to deem the import of the red-eared slider illegal. Australia, for its part, has been highly proactive at reducing occurrence of red-eared sliders in their territory. Harsh penalties for its illegal import have been accompanied by ongoing eradication measures, awareness programs and the labelling of red-eared slider turtle as a Class 1 pest.

To make matters more complicated, should you choose to simply go looking for red-eared slider eggs or hatchlings in the wild, or give a home to a lost pet, ensure that you are legally permitted to do so. Many states prohibit their residents to adopt red-eared sliders, owing to the complications behind rehabilitating a chelonian, and for fear of the owner contracting salmonella, or releasing the pet back into the wild.

The question then arises, "can I legally own a red-eared slider at all in the United States?" If you're willing to be diligent about adhering to local wildlife laws, in many areas, you most certainly can. A quick perusal of the local Game and Wildlife laws that govern each county or state reveals it is only those areas most severely impacted by the introduction of the red-eared terrapin into their native ecosystem that have specific guidelines dictating the terms of their sale, acquisition or ownership. Therefore, while you still may not be able to either bring home or raise a red-eared slider in the states of Florida and Oregon, you most certainly can give a home to at least one or two chelonians in other North American states, Canada and Europe – so long as they aren't imported. Consider your purchase as a way of providing long-term help to check the population of invasive species in your local ecosystem, and you may find that owning a red-eared slider turtle is not that tricky a process to navigate.

If you aren't sure whom to ask for the right legal information concerning the acquisition and ownership of red-eared slider turtles as pets, you can find plenty of literature on this subject on the Internet. Each state's government website lists out all particulars surrounding the purchase and possession of its local flora and fauna. Browse through the Game and Wildlife department pages for the most accurate and up-to-date information.

5. The right age and gender to bring home Red-eared Slider Turtles – and how many

Once you have assured yourself – through adequate research and homework – of the legality of bringing home a red-eared slider turtle in your geographic location, you can begin to think about the specifics of your pet. Many potential terrapin owners often find themselves conflicted between the choice to bring home fully-grown adult red-eared sliders or raise baby hatchlings into adults. Your ultimate decision should be one that addresses the purposes behind bringing home your chelonian.

The first factor to bear in mind is the nature of your pet, regardless of their age; red-eared slider turtles live out their existence on two surfaces – water as well as land, requiring both in equal measure to thrive. As the caregiver of a creature whose life cycles determine such basic activities as breathing, nutrient absorption and foraging for food, you have to be ready to usher your pet through each developmental stage.

You then turn to address the purpose of the new pet in your household - are they your first chelonian or turtle, or are they brought to add to an already existing community? If this is your first experience with handling and caring for exotic reptiles, it may be preferable to bring adult birds, and care for the young when subsequent eggs are laid.

This does not mean that young red-eared sliders should not be considered at the time of purchase - simply that they require more exacting care than their adult counterparts. If you happen to acquire, or wish to purchase red-eared slider turtles, therefore, it is best that you make arrangements for an aquatic environment with a designated dry area for basking, essential for younger hatchling development. A largely protein-rich carnivorous diet, the right temperature settings and privacy should help your young one grow into a beautiful sexually mature adult within 2-7 years, depending on the gender.

It must be remembered, however, that the 4-inch law that restricts the sale of turtles in the United States may either make it legally complicated, or next-to-impossible to bring home a young red-eared slider turtle. If you find yourself faced with no choice but to bring home a maturing or fully-matured adult red-eared terrapin, you can still enjoy a lasting and fulfilling relationship with the pet, so long as you can provide lasting care and attention.

If you already have your own community of red-eared sliders at home, hatchlings may not easily blend into an already evolved environment. An adult community of red-eared terrapin requires an adult to properly adapt to the generally aggressive initiation ritual and subsequent competition for food and mates. While your society of red-eared sliders may shun and even bully younger hatchlings, they are more likely to treat an adult of similar size with higher tolerance.

The true dilemma in bringing home a solitary red-eared slider lies in the eventual need to provide it with a partner. While not particularly intent on breeding or reproducing, red-eared sliders have been studied to thrive emotionally when provided with at least one other companion. Whether of complementary or contrasting genders, it is the social interaction that keeps the turtles from exhibiting highly fearful and aggressive behaviour patterns.

As an amateur breeder, it would do you best to begin with one turtle, and work your way towards investing in a tank mate;

should you have the resources and patience, however, consider bringing home a pair from the get go. Apart from the slight increase in your initial investments, you will have a higher likelihood of bringing home pets that get along.

As with many animal species, a male and female adult would ideally do well if housed together. Two males may only compete during the rare feeding or basking ritual, and a pair of females have been studied to get along splendidly. In case of a community setting, however, it may be best to either have a larger number of females in the tank, or house the males and females separately at the time of breeding and mating to avoid competitive or sexually aggressive behaviour towards each other.

No matter what the age of the red-eared slider you ultimately do bring home, it is essential that the animal be in as healthy a state as possible. Have your reptile tested for salmonella and any other existing medical conditions, and give an initial period of at least 30 days in quarantine, till they adapt to their surroundings.

6. The Pros and Cons of Red-eared Slider turtle ownership

Pros of Red-eared slider turtle ownership

As an exotic semi-aquatic invasive species, red-eared slider turtles may not have the universal appeal that dogs and cats command as prized pets. They demand exacting living, behavioral, diet and health conditions in order to thrive, and take relatively longer to tame than other popular pet species. For those who follow a routine that complements the animal's diurnal natures and can make the commitment, however, raising pet red-eared terrapins can turn into a therapeutic and rewarding experience. Despite their slightly distant nature's, red-eared slider turtles can be advantageous to their caregivers in the following ways:

• Diurnal by nature, red-eared slider turtles are active by day and asleep during the night hours, making them easy to bond with if you work from home or are free during the daytime.

• While in their tank, they are agile swimmers, making them entertaining to watch. They can be tamed to an extent and once you forge a bond with your terrapins, you can also expect them to be responsive to your presence.

• The most popular pet among the semi-aquatic turtle family, red-eared sliders have maintained interactions with humans since the 1900s, making them relatively friendlier towards humans than the yellow-bellied or Cumberland slider turtles.

• Red-eared slider turtles may grow to a size of up to 10 inches, but are also among the smaller-size of the semi-aquatic and basking turtle family. If you are looking to domesticate a turtle that does not demand overly large enclosures and too much space, the red-eared slider would be a better option than the yellow-bellied slider or cooter turtle.

• With a need for a specific temperature and habitat setting that can be provided in an enclosed space through such simple devices as water heaters and basking lamps, you can comfortably house red-eared slider turtles through a variety of climatic conditions.

• Depending on the hygiene standards housing you provide, red-eared sliders can be hardy little creatures, with immune systems that can resist several infections - health problems, if any, will often result from shell-related ailments, or wounds and bites sustained from injuries.

• For those looking to bring home a pet that does not require excessive handling and is meant for decorative purposes, the red-eared slider turtle is an attractive and non-threatening option when compared to such exotic pets as snakes, lizards and certain frogs, and adds an aesthetic touch to the spaces it inhabits.

• For those looking to bring home a pet that can be housed inside an aquarium, red-eared slider turtles make for a longer-living and hardier option than most freshwater fish, while also being more responsive than several popular pet fish species.

• Red-eared slider turtles are also an excellent option for those people looking to provide a home for a displaced or neglected exotic pet – you can find plenty of healthy red-eared sliders up for adoption at veterinary facilities, re-homing and animal rescue centres.

• With a preference for privacy and relative solitude, red-eared sliders do not require daily bonding and playtime in order to thrive. As long as you can provide food, clean water and optimum basking conditions on a daily basis, your red-eared sliders will not demand extra attention from you – making them a better option than such pets as chipmunks or dogs.

• When compared to many other pets, red-eared slider turtles live a relatively long life of 20 to 30 years in captivity, sometimes even making it for over half a century! This longevity of existence makes them ideal pet for those who become quickly attached to their pets and are looking for lifetime domestic companionship.

Cons of Red-eared slider turtle ownership

Among those who have not raised a turtle, cold-blooded or aquatic pet, or any type of exotic before, it is a common misconception that these chelonians with a pleasing appearance are low-maintenance and require little care. This harboured notion, however, could not be further from the truth. As is common with all exotics, red-eared slider turtles, too, display behavior patterns that are different from other conventional pets such as dogs, cats, rabbits or horses. They are less likely to adapt their lifestyle to suit yours; rather it is you whose schedule will have to complement the terrapin's in order for it to survive. As companionable as they can be in the home of the right owner, here are some of the ways through which red-eared slider turtles could become a disadvantage to unprepared or unwilling owners:

• Red-eared slider turtles are not needy, but can be highly dependent on their caregiver as pets. Apart from timely feeding and health check-ups, you will also have to devote scheduled time on a daily, weekly and monthly basis towards cleaning their enclosure.

• While content to be among their kind as adults, they demand a high level of attention from caregivers as hatchlings. The process of hatchling red-eared slider eggs, as well as caring for them through their first year requires patience and diligence.

• Despite relying on their caregiver for food, basking and hygiene housing in captivity, red-eared slider turtles are fiercely independent by nature, preferring to be touched or held only when they please. You may spend hours each day caring for and watching your red-eared slider turtles, and the chelonian may still be averse to your touch, or may resist being held.

• Red-eared slider turtles may be content to be house within a controlled environment, but are also relatively messy animals who will dirty their surroundings on a daily basis. You will need to make provisions for daily water filtering, spot-cleaning and habitat overhauling on a regular basis to prevent infections and disease from contaminating the housing.

• Personality-wise, red-eared slider turtles can become defensive during such times as feeding, mating or nesting, towards their tank mates as well as their caregivers. Pet owners often narrate tales of their pets regularly displaying varying degrees of dominance and aggression towards other mates or the caregiver themselves, based on their individual personalities.

• Red-eared sliders turtles are known to bite, kick or scratch other tank mates, or even their caregiver. It must be noted, however, that these pets will seldom bite without reason - if they do, it is most often an instinctual response to be held or touched.

• If you are looking for a pet who can be limited to the confines of their tank without added security measures, do not be fooled by the red-eared slider's laid-back demeanor and small size. Curious by nature, they will wander off if their tanks or housing if left unlocked or uncovered. They are also prized targets for common predators found in an urban setting and can easily be attacked by a dog, cat, fox, snake or even another large turtle.

• Red-eared sliders can also be stubborn pets who are indifferent towards instructions, making their training somewhat exhausting for the caregiver.

• Requiring constant monitoring of their habitat, along with scheduled cleaning, caring for red-eared sliders can limit such activities as taking holidays or long trips away from home, unless an alternate caregiver is found.

• With such needs as water filtration devices, basking zones and lamps, water heating products and regular upkeep of enclosure, providing an ideal setting for your red-eared slider turtles can quickly become a costly affair, making them an unsuitable option for those on a tight budget.

• If you are unsure of the caregiver's ability or preference to care for a pet for at least 20 years, the longevity of this chelonians life may be a disadvantage to such potential owners as children.

• Their status as invasive species and the legalities placed on the breeding, sale and release of red-eared sliders in the wild makes it difficult for red-eared sliders to be re-homed in case you find yourself overwhelmed by the expenses and time that they take up.

7. The amount of work involved

A variety of factors come into play when determining whether a red-eared slider turtle - or two - will be suitable as a pet for you. We have already discussed, at length, the amount of considerations you are required to make as a caregiver - from understanding the legal and social implications of housing this invasive terrapin species, to learning what caring for this reptile truly entails. In order to properly summarize all the prerequisites that are best fulfilled before acquiring a red-eared slider turtle, here is a checklist of questions to ask yourself:

• Can you comfortably set aside between 800 and 1500 USD (500-1000 British pounds) every year for the care and upkeep of your pet?

• Can you fulfil all the legal requisites placed by your local authorities before owning a red-eared slider turtle?

• Can you comfortably and consistently source and provide live feed, plant matter, vegetables and water that is clean and filtered and changed regularly?

• Can you locate a reputed and trustworthy exotic pet care expert/veterinarian in your area for your chelonian?

• Can you efficiently make the premises within the housing zone ideal for your red-eared slider, with designated areas for swimming, basking, feeding and burrowing?

• Can you efficiently make the premises outside the tank "predator-and-injury-proof" before it's time to let your red-eared slider out for optional sunlight and exercise?

• Can you dedicatedly spare time once a day to spot clean the tank, and then clear time once or twice a month for a complete clean-up and overhaul?

• Can you be patient and handle being constantly nipped, kicked or scratched - especially during the first few weeks?

• Can you devote ample time and space on a daily basis towards basking and swimming for its enrichment and wellbeing?

• Can you live with a chelonian who may develop an aggressive personality, or who may abhor being touched or handled?

• Can you comfortably handle a turtle when it becomes temperamental and calm it down?

• Are you ready to handle aggressive impulses, antisocial phases or an indifferent attitude from your pets, especially during the winter and breeding months?

• Can you quickly spot and address any health-related issues that many crop up in your red-eared sliders?

• Can you either prevent or control breeding among your red-eared sliders, or provide a home for all resulting hatchlings?

• Can you provide care for your pet from a responsible person in your absence?

• Are you comfortable with caring for a pet for at least 20 and maybe up to 50 or more years?

• Can you provide dedicated care for the pet throughout its lifespan, without subjecting it to the wild or giving it up for adoption?

No matter how the above list of questions may guide your final decision, ultimately, bringing home a red-eared slider turtle should be a decision that enhances the lives of both, the amphibian, and you.

Chapter 4: Acquiring your Red-eared slider Turtle

Once you have put careful thought into the consequences that bringing home a red-eared slider turtle can have, it is best to find the right sources to purchase your pet from. Buying a red-eared slider turtle takes more effort than walking into a shop and selecting the prettiest reptile on a whim; a variety of factors determine whether the red-eared slider turtle on offer is in good enough condition to take home with you. When you set out to buy a red-eared slider turtle, aim to return with the healthiest terrapin of the bunch. You can only receive a complete bill of health from your local chelonian expert, but a few simple physical indicators should reveal the state of health of your prospective red-eared slider turtle:

1. The eyes of the red-eared slider turtle should be clear, and not clouded over, sunken or oozing any liquids,
2. A healthy red-eared slider turtle hatchling can walk almost immediately after it hatches, and swim 21 days after hatching. Any hatchling that is lethargic or immobile is unhealthy,
3. The red-eared slider turtle should either be actively swimming and basking during the day hours, not resting or floating listlessly around the tank; any irregular motor movement signals injury, even deformity,
4. The shell should be smooth, elongated and have a keel in the centre; any cracks, moldy growth, foul smell or bleeding is a sign of fatal injury.
5. A healthy red-eared slider turtle will constantly look for food sources; lack of appetite is an indicator of poor health,
6. While red-eared slider turtles are messy, they are not unhygienic. If the prospective red-eared slider turtle is covered in his own fecal matter, which is alarmingly

smelly, or is covered in mites, the red-eared slider turtle is not   healthy.

7. Ensure that the nose is not runny or swollen, as this may indicate an infection that the red-eared slider turtle will carry for life and possibly spread to other birds.

8. Finally, check the red-eared slider turtle for visible injuries, scars, sores or wounds. Only if the red-eared slider turtle can clear all your health inspection should you ask the vendors for the price.

1. Buying a Red-eared Slider Turtle from a Vendor

The most easily available source of red-eared slider turtles for purchase are reputed and licensed pet stores in your area. Sliders available at these stores are often sold at a lower rate than other sources such as breeders and fanciers, often because they have been acquired in large numbers at wholesale rates, or possibly even rescued from adoption homes. Many stores also have online portals that allow you to select and have your red-eared slider shipped to your location for an extra charge.

Red-eared sliders acquired from pet stores may also not be as tame or friendly as those purchased from breeders and fanciers, as potential taming requires the caregiver to personally devote time and attention to each animal. This may not be possible for a pet store owner to achieve on a daily basis. Lack of individual attention and personalized attention towards feeding and health care rituals may also result in the red-eared slider becoming stressed and falling ill before it reaches you.

Those red-eared sliders who are housed together in cramped quarters without adequate space for basking or swimming also tend to hold on to their aggressive natures in order to survive. Constant scuffles with other companions may also lead to injuries, infections and possible deformities in the chelonians. If your selected red-eared slider has had to compete with other tank mates for space and food for a prolonged period, it may be almost impossible to completely tame them. Terrapins who have been acquired from such environments are rarely known to survive past the initial few weeks, let alone become domesticated or form lasting bonds with their caregivers.

If the nearest pet store is located in another town or city, and chooses to ship the red-eared slider to you, the conditions of the shipping container also determine how healthy your pet will be when it arrives at your doorstep. Unless you personally choose your turtle after making an informed decision, buying a red-eared slider from a pet store may not always be the wisest choice in the long-term.

When you visit the pet store to select your pet, it's best to have at least a basic idea of how to differentiate between a male and female red-eared slider, as well as prepare a mental checklist of signs of a healthy red-eared slider. While examining the red-eared slider turtles to select a suitable candidate, here are some probable instances at the pet store that should raise red flags and cause you to reconsider your purchase:

• The dealer cannot differentiate between a male and female red-eared slider,

• The dealer has no knowledge of the age, shell-measurement, breed or legal requirements of red-eared slider turtle ownership,

• Many red-eared slider turtles have been housed together in the same quarters, making them cramped,

• The red-eared slider has already begun to show signs of distress (lethargy, listless or restless behavior) at the store.

If you choose to have your red-eared slider shipped or are making your purchase online, ensure that the pet store or online retailer has a return or money-back policy in place, in case you are dissatisfied with your pet. The above red flags also apply to red-eared slider turtles who are shipped to your premises. In addition, you should also be wary if:

• The shipping crates shown to you have no burrowing spaces,

• The dealer makes plans to ship the red-eared slider turtles during the daytime - despite the red-eared slider turtles being diurnal. Activity such as being transported across borders during their waking hours will prevent the red-eared slider turtles from falling asleep and cause stress, agitation, even illness.

2. Buying a Red-eared Slider Turtle from a Breeder

They may not be as easy to find as pet stores and online retailers, but if you are keen on bringing home a healthy red-eared slider, locating your nearest reputed red-eared slider breeder might be a safer and wiser option. Breeders are people who raise red-eared slider turtles for sale and profit, often caring for more than one generation at a time.

Raising red-eared slider turtles to appeal to potential caregivers forms the livelihood of breeders; they, therefore, take great pains to provide the right kind of care to the chelonians - be it housing them in spacious aquatic settings, providing timely - and ample - nutritious food, and ensuring that each red-eared slider receives individual medical attention. Breeders also house red-eared slider turtles in compatible groups, pairings and species, allowing you to pick up multiple exotics with greater chances of the red-eared slider turtles getting along in case of a community set-up. Those professionals who specialize in red-eared slider turtles will often also take an interest in raising other turtle breeds, such as yellow-bellied slider turtles, Cumberland sliders, boxed turtles, painted turtles and the like, to widen your options.

Due to the exhaustive effort contributed towards raising healthy and viable red-eared slider turtles, the cost of purchasing a pet from a breeder may be a little higher than the rate offered by your neighborhood pet store. What you will receive in exchange for this extra sum, however, is a red-eared slider with superior breeding, a positive social disposition than wild counterparts and relatively good health. Breeders will also possess sufficient knowledge of the 4-inch law and other legalities, and will be able to accurately pinpoint each variety of red-eared slider out to you. They will also have records of the date of birth, breed, vaccinations, necessary permits and possibly even lineage, to share with you.

Many breeders take a personal interest in their red-eared slider turtles and like to ensure that they end up in a safe and loving house that can promise lifelong care. They also have hands-on experience at caring for red-eared slider turtles, and are often good sources of information on pet care. Thorough professionals at their job, breeders will be able to properly advise on the individual personality quirks of each reptile, can help you find reputed food and housing resources, and can also refer you to a trusted exotic pet expert for healthcare.

Breeders, especially those raising such invasive species as red-eared sliders, are always looking for potential caregivers for their exotics, and will place advertisements on such platforms as newspaper classifieds, community newsletters and message boards, or even on the Internet. While largely an honest and hardworking group of people, you may still encounter the odd breeder whose concerns are more monetary than emotional. They may not have set out in the effort to raise tame red-eared slider turtles, or may have ignored their health and welfare, but will still quote rates that most top-quality breeders charge. It is best to make a personal visit to the breeder if you can, before you make your purchase, in order to assess the quality of care provided to the red-eared slider turtles, as well as the trustworthiness of the seller.

3. Buying a Red-eared Slider Turtle from previous owners

Fanciers are often confused with breeders since they are individuals who usually advertise red-eared slider turtles for sale from their homes. The main difference between fanciers and breeders, however, is that fanciers chance upon red-eared slider babies when their own pets lay a clutch that they are unable to raise themselves upon hatching. Often an unexpected surprise to the owners, red-eared slider turtles acquired from fanciers may only be of a certain variety or coloring, limiting your choices.

Since fanciers are not professional breeders, they are often not required to possess any certification or licenses confirming their status as sellers. This can make them challenging to locate; their information won't be found on community pet forums or with reputed veterinarians. If they do have a chelonian for sale, however, fanciers will advertise through local media, and can be contacted accordingly.

Rare though these pets may be, red-eared slider turtles acquired from fanciers are likely to have a healthier disposition than their store-bought and professionally-bred counterparts. These red-eared slider turtles are raised in a domestic environment, and are comfortable with human interaction from the start. These red-eared slider turtles also receive individual attention and care from their caregivers, making them more likely to form a bond with you. Fanciers can also be reliable sources of advice and point you towards the best veterinarian, food brands and housing options for your pets.

On the flip side, fanciers, being individual owners, may not always possess the legal authority to either raise hatchlings, or sell them under the prohibitions exercised by the 4-inch law. In addition, some fanciers may not want to sell you young red-eared sliders at all; instead, they may try to pass off ageing, unwanted adults as prospective pets. To avoid such mishaps, it is best that you pay a personal visit to the fancier, and verify their credibility with local exotic pet communities, if possible.

4. Finding a Red-eared Slider Turtle in the wild

In areas that form their natural range, red-eared slider turtles can easily be spotted at the edge of river bank areas, at private muddy clearings, and even in the gardens and backyards of many residential settlements. Depending on whether they were raised in the wild, or let out by previous owners from a captive state, the red-eared slider turtles may be governed by laws restricting their possession, ownership and displacement from their habitat. If you chance upon a red-eared slider in the wild, it is important to understand that it cannot be picked and domesticated using the same techniques employed for a stray dog or cat.

As exotic cold-blooded reptiles, red-eared slider turtles will not become domesticated upon initial human contact. It takes weeks, even months of behavioral therapy from professionally-trained rehabbers to adapt red-eared slider turtles rescued from the wild into captivity. As an amateur caregiver, you may not have the resources or the patience to provide such exacting care.

Transitioning from the wild to a captive state will require the red-eared slider to learn new foraging, basking and cohabitation patterns, adapt to an unfamiliar housing environment, and accept novel behavior patterns from strangers not usually interacted with in their natural history. Without necessary education on the matter, trying to rehabilitate a red-eared slider on your own may turn quickly stressful, both for you and the animal.

Wild red-eared slider turtles may also be carriers of salmonella, especially if they are found with a shell length of less than 4 inches, as per United States Wildlife law, and may infect humans during interaction. Furthermore, acquiring a red-eared slider from the wild is strictly prohibited by several states across the United States with ownership and acquisition banned in two, and is punishable by hefty fines. If found abandoned in the wild, red-eared slider turtles are either best left alone, or rushed to the nearest exotic pet centre for medical attention and rehabilitation. For the purposes of purchase, it is wise to stick with reputed and reliable sources as breeders, fanciers and adoption homes for displaced or abandoned pets and exotics - these will provide you with red-eared slider turtles who have had prior exposure to human contact and will be easy to tame and bond with.

5. Buying Red-eared Slider Turtles in the UK and USA

Even though red-eared slider turtles may be most easily available through local pet stores, if you do not wish to adopt your pet from a trusted adoption home, it is advisable to buy such exotic pets from more reputed sources like breeders. Whether you live in the United States or United Kingdom, breeders are often trusted more than any other source to sell potential owners pets who have been legally acquired, tamed and vaccinated.

If you live in the United States, most breeders and fanciers will place advertisements for red-eared sliders for sale on such websites as Exotic Animals for Sale or Domestic Sale. In the United Kingdom, red-eared sliders for sale can be found on websites as Preloved and Pets4Homes.

6. Initial Check-ups and Vaccinations

Regardless of the source through which you purchase your red-eared sliders, it is essential that they receive medical attention before they are brought home. Depending on the care provided to your terrapins before its sale, you may need to verify that your pet has no underlying illnesses or infections; you may also have to administer a dose of initial vaccinations.

As we have already discussed, red-eared slider turtles can be potential carriers of salmonella, apart from other infections. If brought home with verification, casual contact with the pet may lead to salmonella spreading among your family members. A simple test at the veterinary office can help prevent long-term lethal effects among your loved ones.

Technically, captive red-eared sliders have been studied to be less-likely carriers of salmonella than their wild counterparts. Developed countries like the United States and United Kingdom have managed to keep the spread of salmonella under control through strict laws, medication and awareness programs, reducing the risk of your pet – or you – being affected.

Red-eared sliders that have been acquired from breeders and fanciers are often healthy and have already been given their course of veterinary check-ups and treatment. In the event that they haven't, your breeder or fancier will usually inform you in advance. To prevent any chance of bringing home a potential host for salmonella, however, ensure that you ask your breeder or fancier for the necessary health certificates proving that your turtle has been medically certified. This certification does not promise that your turtle will be salmonella-free through its lifetime, but will prevent illness from entering your house at the time of purchase.

Other sources such as pet store vendors may or may not have their red-eared sliders medically certified; the care provided to pets within a store is usually determined by the dedication of the vendor towards selling healthy specimen. Terrapins acquired from pet stores may also have sustained injuries or contracted respiratory or eye infections from other members in the tank that are not instantly visible. To avoid any such mishaps, it is best to make an appointment with a reputed exotic pet expert for an initial round of check-ups on the day that your purchase your red-eared slider turtle.

7. Can Red-eared Slider Turtles be electronically tagged?

Ideally, a domesticated pet should be loyal to its immediate surroundings, and not venture too far from their homes. In the case of such pets as dogs or cats, adequate training and care is usually enough to ensure that the pet does not run away. As exotics pets, however, red-eared slider turtles, though they can be tamed, cannot always be prevented from escaping their cages and out of the house through an open door or window.

Curious and independent by nature, even the most tame red-eared slider will usually want to explore its immediate surroundings, usually for food, and could easily become lost. Devices such as embedded microchips act as tracking equipment to help return lost and found pets to their owners. In addition, the microchips can also record such information as the breed of the animals and the vaccinations provided, helping your veterinarian monitor your pet's care more efficiently.

Electronic tags are most commonly suggested for such animals as dogs, cats, and those domestic breeds who have been raised for profit, such as goats and chickens. However, electronic tagging is not restricted to certain species of animals; it is, in fact, recommended among as many domesticated pets, whether conventional or exotic, as possible.

Not much larger than a grain of rice, an electronic microchip is available in different models and can easily be inserted by a reputed veterinarian with a simple procedure, should you choose to have your pet electronically tagged. With the site of injection varying depending on the species of animal, most turtles and tortoises often have tag inserted in the hind left limb with some tissue glue used to seal the skin together. This procedure is also relatively painless, and will hurt your chelonian only as much as the prick of a needle would.

Most pet stores and breeders across the United States and United Kingdom choose to have pets such as dogs and cats electronically tagged, but this requirement may vary among exotic pet breeders and vendors. As with vaccinations, it is best to check with your breeder if your pet has been tagged, as ownership details on the microchip will have to be transferred under your name and address.

If your red-eared slider turtle has not been microchipped, you can acquire the electronic tagging through such websites as ID Tag, and Smart chip. Once embedded, your pet's details can be registered with such companies as PetKey and Pet Protect - most registration websites recognize all popular electronic tagging brands, making the identification, monitoring and tracking of your turtle hassle-free and convenient.

Chapter 5: Housing your Red-eared Slider Turtle

1. Setting up a house for your Red-eared Slider Turtle

When setting up the housing area for your turtles, you will have to firstly consider the size of the tank intended to house the pets. This size is determined by the number of red-eared sliders you will house together, along with the age and gender of the turtles at the time of acquisition. Ideally, you should intend to keep a pair of adult red-eared terrapins per enclosure, preferably a male and his female counterpart.

You will find that a tank with a volume of approximately 60 gallons houses one or two growing red-eared sliders comfortably. If a pair of adults is your initial purchase, or you intend to raise the hatchlings within the same tank, it will then need a volume of at least 80 gallons for an adult male slider, while a full grown female will need a 125-gallon tank for comfortable housing.

If you still find yourself unsure of the adequate volume of the tank for your individual turtle, try this calculation trick adopted by several turtle owners and breeders: 10 gallons for every square inch of your terrapin's shell should guide towards picking a tank with a capacity between 75 and 125 gallons.

Apart from the conventional glass or acrylic aquariums that may be popularly advertised as ideal housing options for red-eared sliders, there exist a couple of alternatives that can just as comfortable, while also being economical to purchase and maintain. Among the most commonly recommended housing enclosures for red-eared slider turtles include:

Plastic stock tanks

Advantages	Disadvantages	Ideal Usage
Relatively cheaper than glass aquarium. Suitable for indoor and outdoor housing. Built especially to store water; ideal aquatic setting for turtles. Opaque black/grey walls offer privacy. Will support lighting, heating, filters and other fixtures. Highly durable; will last longer than other housing options	Not as attractive as glass aquarium. Opaque walls offer no view of turtles within.	Can be bought from farm supply stores. Should be covered with canopy, screen covering or similar roof to prevent escape and regulate lighting. If used as outdoor housing, can also support drainage features

Perfomed / Custom ponds

Advantages	Disadvantages	Ideal Usage
Highly customizable housing option that allows for personalization. Ideal for outdoor housing. Relatively durable compared to glass aquariums. Relatively cheaper than glass aquariums. Built for water storage. Can house separate basking and nesting areas within same space. Can support heating, lighting, filtering fixtures.	Requires more thought and labor to set up than other housing. Not ideal for indoor housing without adequate support.	Best if used for outdoor housing at ground level. If housing indoors, incorporate pond liner around the edges

Plastic Storage containers

Advantages	Disadvantages	Ideal Usage
Considerably cheaper than aquarium. Opaque/translucent walls offer privacy. Lightweight, portable, durable. Available in many shapes and sizes.	Less attractive than a glass aquarium. Requires additional support when filled with water. May develop cracks leading to water seepage.	Opt for darker toned containers; avoid bright colors. Provide support with wooden or PVC frames or braces. Regulate and monitor water and temperature. Opt for clamp-style lighting

Regulating the Temperature

The right temperature conditions within your red-eared slider's housing zone makes a lot of difference between your pet surviving and thriving. With a narrow window of ideal temperatures that governs such basic responses as swimming, encouraging appetite and even sex determination among these chelonians, it becomes your responsibility to ensure the housing area can provide such a favourable setting in captivity.

In the wild, these terrapins exist comfortably in ambient temperatures that range between 75-80 F (24-27 C). Requiring devoted time both, on land and in water, an aquatic temperature between 75-78 F (23-26 C) and a basking zone temperature of 90-95 F (32-35 C) would be ideal. Should you bring home red-eared slider hatchlings, the temperature of the water will have to be maintained at 78-80 F (26-27 C) for the first 12 months.

In captivity, red-eared slider turtles have curiously been observed to do better at higher temperatures than colder ones. This could be due to their instinctual preference for the slightly tropical and warmer climates that promotes such activities as basking, feeding, swimming and general activity. Lower temperature, on the other hand, is observed the red-eared slider turtle during the cooler hours of the day and the winter months – a time of brumation and relative inactivity. However, it is essential that this regulated temperature be consistently maintained, so as not to place your red-eared terrapins under physical or emotional duress.

When exposed to prolonged bouts of heat for days at a time, red-eared slider turtles may come under duress, and become severely dehydrated. If left exposed to cold temperatures or chilly draft from exposed vents for prolonged periods, your terrapins experience loss of appetite, lethargy and listlessness and may even develop pneumonia. It is best to place a thermometer attached to each specialized zone within the tank so you can accurately monitor the conditions within the aquatic and basking areas.

If you live in cooler climates, and find that you need to provide additional heat sources for the tank, it is best to invest in submersible water heaters. These devices, when immersed underwater, can raise gently the temperature of the surroundings without abruptly disturbing the turtle. You can control how much heat is provided from any point of the tank by positioning your water heaters away from the basking zones – this prevents a drastic rise in the temperature settings.

Red-eared slider turtles rely largely on the moisture in their environment to provide them with hydration. For these purposes, it becomes your responsibility to ensure that the tank is always filled with enough water, and that the temperature settings maintain optimum humidity. Sufficient ventilation is also essential for the maintenance of a regulated temperature within the tank. It is essential that clean oxygen be allowed to circulate around the housing area without giving the terrapins the opportunity to slip out of their homes. You can accomplish this by covering the top of the tank with a wire mesh screen fitting. A poorly ventilated tank may not only become over-heated, but will also evolve into a hotspot for disease and infections.

Providing ideal lighting conditions

Lighting plays almost more of a crucial role than other factors that determine the ideal housing for your chelonians. Cold-blooded and diurnal by nature, red-eared slider turtles rely on the comforting warmth and light from the sun's rays for their daily basking activities. An indoor setting may not always allow unfiltered sunrays to seep through the tank; this makes it necessary to invest in the right lighting fixture alternatives for reptilian housing.

Most forms of conventional lighting will also impart some amount of heat, making a difference to the overall temperature of the tank. If the temperature of the housing area is already strictly regulated, any further damaging heat from the lighting may only cause stress to the pets. However, should you house any live plants in the tank along with the red-eared sliders, then some form of artificial lighting then becomes essential. Without any source of light, the turtles will become unable to bask on a daily basis, while plants in the tank, unable to process food, will subsequently die. The best lighting solutions for such housing conditions have been found to be UVA and UVB lighting fixtures, preferably low-wattage (5 or 10 %) fluorescent tubes. This form of lighting manages to impart light that is absorbed by the plants without emitting any extra heat.

UVA lighting has been studied to have positive psychological benefits among chelonians, while UVB lighting, even when provided through an artificial source, helps the turtle absorb and convert vitamin D3, essential for physical development. In addition, UVB lighting does not illuminate the entire space, leaving the turtles with darker aquatic areas, should they feel uncomfortable with excessive light. It is best to place the lights in a corner at an angle at the basking zone, rather than fix them flat and centre at the roof of the tank. This setting will further separate designated areas in your tank, putting your pets at ease.

The nature of the lighting should also mimic the daily cycle of the red-eared slider turtles. This chelonian usually spends about 12 hours of the day needing strong light, choosing to bask when the light and heat are at their strongest. Try to regulate the lighting to be on when the pet needs it, and off when your turtle is ready to rest.

Assessing the Water requirements of the Tank

Whether they spend most of their day swimming, or choose to bask on the terrestrial side of the tank, red-eared slider turtles, like all semi-aquatic pond-dwellers, require a body of water in their premises in order for them thrive. As animals reliant on water as a source of transport, food, hydration and even mating, an abundant source of water in their surroundings becomes doubly important.

For a pair of growing red-eared slider hatchlings, a tank set-up with a volume of 40-60 gallons should be sufficient. If you are raising your hatchlings into fully grown adults, on the other hand, or are bringing home solely adult red-eared slider turtles, you will need to invest in a tank set-up that can comfortably hold at least 125 gallons for a pair of fully-grown females.

While you may require such a large tank set-up to contain your chelonians, you definitely will not be immersing them entirely in an underwater environment! The amount of water you fill into the housing area largely depends on your discretion. The only factor to bear in mind is that the depth of the water be enough to allow your red-eared slider to submerge itself. As a rule of thumb, the depth of the water should ideally be 2 times the length of the turtle's shell: By these calculations, a turtle with a 4-inch shell will require water that is about 8 inches deep.

No matter how much of your pet housing space is taken up by water, ensure that it is as clean and fresh as possible. Most red-eared slider turtles adapt perfectly well to regular tap water, kept at room temperature and regulated at the right setting within the tank, provided the water is free of any traces of chlorine. Chlorine has been studied to have a level of negative effects among these chelonians, no matter how small, and in combination with other chemicals in tap water, may become potentially illness-inducing for your pet.

Chelonian breeders and owners have noticed that fresh rainwater also seems to be well-suited for the tank, provided this water has not been stagnant before collection. Stagnant rainwater is a breeding hotspot for germs, bacteria and viruses, and is inadvisable as an addition to your controlled ecosystem. You may think to use distilled water, but this may also be an unwise option. Distilled water is usually over-treated to the point where it is stripped off essential minerals that the terrapins will need. Bottled spring water is an ideal choice, but is too laughably expensive an option to consider for most potential owners.

If it is difficult or inconvenient for you to provide rainwater for your tank, you can undertake a simple de-chlorination process by treating your water with a water conditioning kit. These inexpensive products are easily available at most local pet stores and markets, and have been especially designed to draw out traces of chlorine, another related particle known as chloramine, as well as any heavy metals.

To ensure that the water content within the housing area is clean and fresh for as long as possible, ensure that you invest in water filters for your aquarium, and have them running at least once daily. Do not let the presence of water filters make you negligent; while they may keep the water fresh for longer periods, you will still need to clean up food and excrement particles from the floor, and change the water at least once every 30-45 days.

Adult red-eared slider turtles have been built to swim - and transition into strong and graceful swimmers, making is necessary to ensure that your terrapin is content with the quality of the water in the tank. Water that is left unchecked, unfiltered and unchanged can quickly become a breeding zone for infections and ailments. A cloudy or muddy aquatic environment, on the other hand, may either visually impair your turtles or even cause drowning.

2. Furnishing the housing area

Once a suitable tank is selected, it must be furnished in a way that is aesthetically pleasing as well as functional for the red-eared sliders. There is no limit - or budget - for the amount of accessories that can be added to your housing set-up. Depending on the quality of life you want to provide to your pets, you can set-up a housing environment that is sparse and functional, or abundant and indulgent.

Flooring and Substrate

The first component that you will want to set into the tank may be the right kind of flooring. Interestingly, red-eared sliders will do perfectly well in a tank that has no substrate – aquatic by nature, the only dry area they require is a platform for basking. The absence of a muddy or stony substrate will also discourage such behaviors as hiding and nesting among the terrapins.

However, should you choose it, a substrate that can withhold large amounts of moisture for an extended period of time without becoming too damp and infestation-friendly. This makes a substrate filled with large, smooth flat stone too big for ingestion appealing.

Compiling the flooring of such large stones also allows you to clean the tank efficiently, and provides the perfect support for aquatic plants. What must be avoided in the red-eared slider's substrate, are small gravelly pieces of debris that can be ingested easily. These terrapins enjoy nothing more than poking at the objects in its environment, eating whatever takes its fancy. Pieces of gravel, sharp jagged stones, etc. may become lodged in the chelonians throat or cause rupture in the digestive tract before embedding itself there.

Basking zones

The most essential element in the tank apart from the right amount of water, is a platform or zone specifically reserved for basking. Red-eared sliders will require a significant portion of their waking hours to indulge in basking activities – the light and heat helps them regulate body temperature, while providing their systems with nourishing UVA and UVB rays. The only requisites for an adequate basking zone are that it be at a significant level above the water (to enable dry basking), and that it not be too close to the basking lamps or roof of the tank. Provided your soldier can comfortably climb onto the platform, a basking zone can either be constructed by a broad platform atop large flat stones stacked over each other in the corner of a tank, or can be purchased from your exotic pet store.

Accessories and aquatic plants

After the basics of the tank are taken care of, other elements should all be aimed towards providing exercise, as well as ensuring that the red-eared slider does not become stressed or listless. Filling their waking hours with such activities as feeding, digging, basking, swimming, chasing tank mates and running, accessories in the tank that can add to their standard of living will promote emotional well-being and keep behavioural disorders at bay.

Your tank will please your pet if it contains some nooks, crannies and hiding spots in the water that do not obstruct its movements. Red-eared sliders love to hide and wander about areas with flat, broad bases; these spaces seem to bring them comfort during times of threat. They also add an ornamental and aesthetic appeal to your tank, making it a relaxing sight for your visitors and for you. Invest in such accessories as small logs, driftwood, flat large stones, small rocks etc. Remember that all items will need to be cleaned, washed and sterilized before depositing into the tank.

You can also set up either artificial or even live plants to add beauty and functionality to your tank. Consider, however, that artificial plants will only add decorative value, while live plants will help further the habitat. Not all live plants may be suitable for the tank and red-eared sliders, however, and will all have to be verified as safe for consumption before adding to the environment. Among the most commonly recommended aquatics for a red-eared slider's tank are arrowheads, Common Eel Grass, Water Hyacinth, Canadian Pondweed, Hair Grass, Water Trumpet, Java Fern, Crystalwort, Java Moss and Water Lettuce.

Red-eared sliders housed in captivity are often exposed to unfamiliar surroundings, especially for the first few days in a new owner's house. A tank placed in the corner of a well-lit room with one side preferably facing a wall provides the terrapin with a safe and familiar corner to which they can retreat in times of stress of perceived threat.

3. Maintaining a hygienic housing environment

You may spend large sums of money to provide the best housing conditions for your red-eared slider turtles, but if you cannot provide the time and commitment required to clean and maintain the housing environment, you expose your pets to a variety of possible infections, ailments and emotional duress. Proper hygiene can be maintained within the tank in the following ways:

1. A daily inspection and cleaning of the tank is essential; messy by nature, red-eared slider turtles will constantly cloud the environment with fecal matter, food remains and shed skin particles.

2. The water-filters should be cleaned with lots of water and a brush once or twice a week, and disinfected once a month.

3. The terrapins should be placed in a separate storage tank till the cleaning and disinfecting process is complete, in order to prevent them from contracting allergies or infections from old particles.

4. The tank should be drained of the water, emptied of all elements, washed and wiped clean, and then be sterilized with the help of a rodent-safe disinfectant.

5. Clean and wipe all the accessories, lighting, heating and filtration equipment disinfecting those as necessary.

6. Before you transfer the turtles back into their housing zone, fill the tank with fresh, clean water, running the filter once for an added cleanliness measure.

7. If you have incorporated flooring elements in the tank, ensure that these are washed and disinfected before being replaced. Try to change such materials as gravel and pebbles as often as possible.

8. A good way of telling that it is time to change your water and substrate is when the tank begins emitting a faint yet rank odor. If left unattended, this damp smell may become more intense, signalling the rotting and decomposing of items within.

9. Take special precaution to regulate the lighting, heat and temperature settings before transferring your turtles in after cleaning. Any irregularities in the housing conditions may trigger unwanted episodes of stress.

Chapter 6: Feeding your Red-eared Slider Turtle

1. What to feed your Red-eared Slider Turtle

Essentially, red-eared slider turtles can survive perfectly well on the commercially prepared food that you provide; in fact, this feed has been formulated keeping the dietary requirements of your chelonians in mind. Natural forage or fresh produce usually comprises a smaller portion of the captive red-eared slider's diet, playing the role of nutritional supplements and appetite stimulants.

This does not mean that you eliminate all natural food from your pet's diet. Fond of such foods as live worms, feeder fish, aquatic plants such as duckweed, vegetables and certain fruits, your slider will be delighted to receive the occasional handful of juicy worms or serving of red lettuce leaf, if added to their feed. Red-eared sliders can also be supplied with a constant source of aquatic plants to feed on by adding them to the substrate, provided they are clean of any pesticides or chemicals. As omnivores, the adults will also enjoy a mealworm or two fed to them a couple times a week. Encouraging your red-eared slider turtle to feed on natural forage such as flies, mosquitoes, spiders and worms in their vicinity is an economical way to provide nutrition and control the spread of pests in your area. Not all plants, grasses, fruits and vegetables are safe for a red-eared slider turtle to consume; several plants and foods can cause toxicity, forcing you to restrict their access to vegetation that is compatible with their system. So long as you can exercise some control over the natural food sources available to your pets, natural forage can be an excellent supplement to the chelonians diet and well-being.

Natural Forage

Live feed

They may be content with such vegetarian sources of food such as plants, vegetables, fruits and grasses, but the red-eared sliders' omnivorous nature means that your pets will consume several kinds of meat with equal gusto – especially as growing hatchlings. Live feed in the form of small worms and insects is also essential to help maintain healthy levels of calcium, phosphorus, proteins and vitamins. This is why you may find the remains of the odd cricket or snail that wandered into the turtle's basking zone or dry area.

Live feed sources that are both comfortable for you to handle, and accepted by the red-eared sliders include mealworms, earthworms, krill and crickets, available at bait and pet stores in fresh and dried form. For aquatic feed, such options as tadpoles and different feeder fish breeds are most preferred. You can also feed small cubes of cooked chicken, fish and turkey to your pets, but it is best that the meat is cooked beforehand and provided very sparingly.

Several owners will only provide cooked meat in dry feeding areas as food remains can contaminate the aquatic zone almost immediately. Others eliminate the option of providing such meats as beef and chicken as part of the turtles' nutrition, and stick with tadpoles, feeder fish and worm varieties. All owners, agree, however, that raw mammalian meat is best avoided as part of your turtle's' diet under any circumstances.

Vegetables and Aquatic Plants

Red-eared sliders may not show the same enthusiasm towards all vegetables as they do for live feed and aquatic plants; these are however beneficial in small quantities and should be added to the diet.

Among the accepted vegetables are mustard and collard leaves, red and romaine lettuce leaves, bock choy, kale, dandelion, carrots, beans and squash. Vegetables can be provided raw, but should preferably be chopped into bite-size cubes. Accepting a large portion of vegetables into their diet will often depend on the personality and taste preferences of each individual red-eared slider, so it is best to try out a number of leafy green options with your pets to ascertain their palate. Including such aquatic plants as anacharis, duckweed, frog bit and water hyacinth into their diet will provide nutritional and emotional benefits. You can also introduce such produce as red lettuce and cabbage leaves. provided sparingly. While your pets may develop a taste for lettuce and cabbages leaves, the chemical composition of these foods in excess can cause an upset stomach.

Fruits

Fruits are not usually favored among red-eared slider turtles, mostly because they are not easily found in their natural setting. If possible, you should limit their exposure to sugary and excessively fatty fruits, incorporating other acceptable ones as rare treat in to their diet. Acceptable fruits include grapes, blackberries, kiwis, pineapple pieces, strawberries, melon cubes and raspberries. Some fruits will need to be prepared before feeding to the red-eared slider, in order to avoid choking hazards or unnecessary illnesses.

Bananas can be avoided, and if fed to the pets, should be peeled and chopped up before serving. Apples and oranges are prized foods, but will need to be de-pipped in advance. The stones should be removed from such fruits as peaches, cherries, plums, nectarines and mangoes. The seeds of nectarines, avocados and mangoes, and the skin of avocados in particular, have been studied to be poisonous and cause toxicity in the chipmunks' systems. Apple pips have also been found to be poisonous to some extent.

Commercially Prepared Foods

As beneficial as natural foraging may be for the well-being of your turtle, in a domestic setting, it works best only as a supplement to your pet's diet. Your own settings may not have adequate foraging resources, and the turtle's greedy natures may prompt them to either indulge in overfeeding or consume those items that may be toxic to their health. In addition, red-eared sliders, based on their individual preferences and personalities, may also display an indifference or aversion towards some vegetables and fruits, healthy though they may be.

You can ensure that your pet's daily dietary needs are met by incorporating commercially prepared feed such as turtle pellets into mealtimes. Not only is turtle feed regarded as beneficial for red-eared sliders in captivity, but is also considered essential for the optimum development of young hatchlings.

Besides containing carefully calculated quantities of your red-eared slider's daily nutritional requirement, commercially-manufactured feed is also formulated to have distinct flavours and tastes, giving your pet a host of culinary options at feeding times. Through trial and error, you, as an owner, can pick from such reputed brands as Purina AquaMax, Mazuri Freshwater Turtle Diet, Tetra ReptoMin, Nasco Turtle Brittle, Fluker's Aquatic Turtle Diet, HBH Turtle Bites and Nutrafin Turtle Gammarus.

If you have to feed hatchlings and younger members up to a year in age, you have to include significant amounts of tissue-building protein. Ideally, protein forms about 40-50 per cent of a growing red-eared slider's diet, a majority of which can be provided through these commercial feeds. As the turtles age past one year, they can progress to foods that substitute excess protein for other essential nutrients such as calcium and phosphorus.

Most commercially pre-packaged turtle feed can be easily sourced from your local pet stores. A common mistake that amateur owners make is to assume that the feed manufactured for a certain aquatic pet is suitable for all aquatic exotics in general. When selecting feed for your red-eared slider turtle, ensure that is has been prepared for the type of aquatic you wish to raise - fish flakes and pellets, along with feed for other semi-aquatic pets such as ducks are often formulated with different nutritional requirements in mind, and are best avoided for your turtle.

If all else fails, you can always contact your pet vendor, exotic chelonian expert or breeder for advice. These are people who are invested in the health and welfare of red-eared slider turtles, and can correctly guide you towards finding the right feed in your area or preparing your own.

The need for Calcium in Red-eared Slider Turtle feed

Calcium is a vital mineral for any growing animal as it helps to build and fortify bone structure. Red-eared sliders, too require significant amounts of calcium during their developing years. Adult red-eared females in particular, demand a specific and significantly higher supply of calcium for better egg-laying along with shell-maintenance once they reach maturation.

The tricky feature of calcium, however, is that its intake needs to be carefully monitored and regulated. A deficiency of calcium in the feed will result in weaker shell structure among all pets, and brittle eggs among your females. Eggs that are laid may not hatch if the turtle's feed has witnessed a deficiency in calcium content. An excess amount of calcium, on the other hand, is just as harmful. You will, therefore, have to be alert towards the amount of calcium your turtles receive in comparison to such minerals as phosphorus or magnesium.

Those members in your tank that do not need large amounts of calcium will find an adequate supply of the mineral in commercially manufactured feed. For those red-eared slider with a calcium deficiency, a mineral source can be provided within the tank for the pet to consume at their convenience.

A potent source of calcium preferred by many pet owners for reptiles is cuttlebone, a rich and common source of calcium. Simply hung in the corner within the tank, your red-eared sliders will have easy access to this calcium source, should they feel lacking. Gut-loaded or calcium-dusted crickets are another popular option and a food favorite with the terrapins. Gut-loaded crickets will require some preparation through careful grinding, crushing and subsequent stuffing of calcium into the abdominal cavities of the crickets, but will make for a perfect calcium supplement.

Since calcium is an essential yet tricky mineral to navigate around, any doubts that you may have regarding its intake should be addressed with your chelonian pet expert. They will be able to correctly guide you and prevent any calcium-related mishaps from occurring within your tank.

2. Check-list of food items acceptable for your Red-eared Slider Turtle

Live feed

1. Crickets:
    Dietary value: dietary staple
    Frequency and preparation: Gut-loaded or dusted
2. Earthworms:
    Dietary value: Supplement to diet
    Frequency and preparation: Fresh, frozen, chopped
3. Silkworms:
    Dietary value: Supplement to diet
    Frequency and preparation: Fresh, frozen, chopped
4. Waxworms:
    Dietary value: Rare treat
    Frequency and preparation: Fresh, frozen, chopped
5. Mealworms:
    Dietary value: Can be avoided
    Frequency and preparation: Fresh, frozen, chopped
6. Super worms:
    Dietary value: Can be avoided
    Frequency and preparation: Fresh, frozen, chopped
7. Tubifex worms:

Dietary value: Can be avoided
Frequency and preparation: Fresh, frozen, chopped

Aquatic Live Feed

1. Guppies:
   Dietary value: Supplement to diet
   Frequency and preparation: Fresh, frozen, chopped
2. Rosy-red minnows:
   Dietary value: Supplement to diet
   Frequency and preparation: Fresh, frozen, chopped
3. Daphnia:
   Dietary value: Supplement to diet
   Frequency and preparation: Fresh, frozen, chopped
4. Krill:
   Dietary value: Rare treat
   Frequency and preparation: Fresh, frozen, chopped, canned
5. Shrimp (Gammarus):
   Dietary value: Rare treat
   Frequency and preparation: Fresh, frozen, chopped, canned
6. Tadpoles:
   Dietary value: Rare treat
   Frequency and preparation: Fresh, frozen, chopped,
7. Apple Snail:
   Dietary value: Rare treat
   Frequency and preparation: Fresh, frozen, chopped, canned
8. Pond Snail:
   Dietary value: Rare treat
   Frequency and preparation: Fresh, frozen, chopped, canned
9. Mosquito larvae:
   Dietary value: Rare treat
   Frequency and preparation: Fresh, frozen, chopped

Aquatic Plants

1. Anacharis:
   Dietary value: Essential
   Frequency and preparation: Fresh, frozen, planted, hand-fed

2. Duckweed:
   Dietary value: Essential
   Frequency and preparation: Fresh, frozen, planted, hand-fed

3. Water Fern:
   Dietary value: Essential
   Frequency and preparation: Fresh, frozen, planted, hand-fed

4. Water Hyacinth:
   Dietary value: Essential
   Frequency and preparation: Fresh, frozen, planted, hand-fed

5. Water Lily:
   Dietary value: Essential
   Frequency and preparation: Fresh, frozen, planted, hand-fed

6. Amazon Swords:
   Dietary value: Staple
   Frequency and preparation: Fresh, frozen, planted, hand-fed

7. Frog bit:
   Dietary value: Staple
   Frequency and preparation: Fresh, frozen, planted, hand-fed

8. Hornwot:
   Dietary value: Staple
   Frequency and preparation: Fresh, frozen, planted, hand-fed

9. Nasturtium:
   Dietary value: Staple
   Frequency and preparation: Fresh, frozen, planted, hand-fed

10. Pondweed:

Dietary value: Staple
Frequency and preparation: Fresh, frozen, planted, hand-fed

11. Water Lettuce:
Dietary value: Staple
Frequency and preparation: Fresh, frozen, planted, hand-fed

12. Water Milofil:
Dietary value: Staple
Frequency and preparation: Fresh, frozen, planted, hand-fed

13. Water Starwort:
Dietary value: Staple
Frequency and preparation: Fresh, frozen, planted, hand-fed

Vegetables and Fruits

1. Dandelion:
Dietary value: Staple
Frequency and preparation: Fresh, raw, chopped

2. Red leaf Lettuce:
Dietary value: Staple
Frequency and preparation: Fresh, raw, chopped

3. Turnip leaves:
Dietary value: Staple
Frequency and preparation: Fresh, raw, chopped

4. Collard greens:
Dietary value: Rare treat
Frequency and preparation: Fresh, raw, chopped

5. Romaine lettuce:
Dietary value: Staple
Frequency and preparation: Fresh, raw, chopped

6. Radicchio:
Dietary value: Rare treat
Frequency and preparation: Fresh, raw, chopped

7. Carrots:
Dietary value: Staple
Frequency and preparation: Fresh, raw, chopped

8. Broccoli:
   Dietary value: Can be avoided
   Frequency and preparation: Fresh, raw, chopped
9. Cabbage:
   Dietary value: Can be avoided
   Frequency and preparation: Fresh, raw, chopped
10. Sweet Potato:
    Dietary value: Staple
    Frequency and preparation: Fresh, raw, chopped
11. Tomatoes:
    Dietary value: Rare treat
    Frequency and preparation: Fresh, raw, chopped
12. Iceberg Lettuce:
    Dietary value: Rare treat
    Frequency and preparation: Fresh, raw, chopped
13. Red Pepper:
    Dietary value: Rare treat
    Frequency and preparation: Fresh, raw, chopped
14. Endive:
    Dietary value: Staple
    Frequency and preparation: Fresh, raw, chopped
15. Kale:
    Dietary value: Staple
    Frequency and preparation: Fresh, raw, chopped
16. Green beans:
    Dietary value: Staple
    Frequency and preparation: Fresh, raw, chopped
17. Beets:
    Dietary value: Can be avoided
    Frequency and preparation: Fresh, raw, chopped
18. Sprouts:
    Dietary value: Can be avoided
    Frequency and preparation: Fresh, raw, chopped
19. Blueberries:
    Dietary value: Rare treat
    Frequency and preparation: Fresh, raw, chopped
20. Blackberries:
    Dietary value: Rare treat

Frequency and preparation: Fresh, raw, chopped

21. Mango:

Dietary value: Staple

Frequency and preparation: Fresh, raw, chopped, peeled

22. Prickly pears:

Dietary value: Staple

Frequency and preparation: Fresh, raw, chopped, de-stemmed

23. Squash:

Dietary value: Staple

Frequency and preparation: Fresh, raw, chopped, peeled, de-stemmed

24. Pumpkin:

Dietary value: Staple

Frequency and preparation: Fresh, raw, chopped, peeled, de-seeded

25. Watermelon

Dietary value: Rare treat

Frequency and preparation: Fresh, raw, chopped, peeled, de-seeded

26. Apple:

Dietary value: Rare treat

Frequency and preparation: Fresh, raw, chopped, peeled, de-seeded

27. Papaya:

Dietary value: Staple

Frequency and preparation: Fresh, raw, chopped, peeled, de-seeded

28. Grapes:

Dietary value: Rare treat

Frequency and preparation: Fresh, raw, chopped, de-seeded

29. Peach:

Dietary value: Rare treat

Frequency and preparation: Fresh, raw, chopped, peeled, de-seeded

30. Cherries:

Dietary value: Rare treat

Frequency and preparation: Fresh, raw, chopped, de-seeded

31. Plums:
    Dietary value: Rare treat
    Frequency and preparation: Fresh, raw, chopped, peeled

32. Banana:
    Dietary value: Rare treat
    Frequency and preparation: Fresh, raw, chopped, peeled

33. Cantalope:
    Dietary value: Staple
    Frequency and preparation: Fresh, raw, chopped

34. Strawberry:
    Dietary value: Rare treat
    Frequency and preparation: Fresh, raw, chopped

Commercial prepacked turtle feed

1. Turtle pellets:
   Dietary value: Staple
   Frequency and preparation: 1 serving = size of turtle head (excluding neck)

2. Processed worms:
   Dietary value: Staple
   Frequency and preparation: Frozen, small serving

3. Processed crickets:
   Dietary value: Staple
   Frequency and preparation: Dried, frozen, gut-loaded

4. Shrimp in brine:
   Dietary value: Rare treat
   Frequency and preparation: Feed as is

5. Frozen feeder fish:
   Dietary value: Staple
   Frequency and preparation: Feed as is

6. Frozen shrimp:
   Dietary value: Rare treat
   Frequency and preparation: Feed as is

7. Frozen krill:
   Dietary value: Rare treat
   Frequency and preparation: Feed as is

8. De-shelled snails:
   Dietary value: Can be avoided
   Frequency and preparation: Feed as is

Miscellaneous food items

1. Canned fish (tuna, salmon):
   Dietary value: Rare treat
   Frequency and preparation: Feed as is
2. Chicken/ turkey meat (cooked):
   Dietary value: Can be avoided
   Frequency and preparation: Cooked, chopped
3. Eggs (boiled):
   Dietary value: Can be avoided
   Frequency and preparation: Cooked, chopped

3. Composition, frequency and healthy feeding habits

Red-eared slider turtles are creatures of summertime foraging and wintertime brumation in the wild. Their appetites and the frequency of feeding seems to be largely reliant on the temperatures in their surroundings; while warmer climates will open up their appetites, cooler temperatures brings about a loss of appetite and the need to shut down and rest. Therefore, you may find yourself feeding the red-eared terrapin with alarming frequency in the summer months, while the winter months may require you to entice them at mealtimes.

Hatchlings, on the other hand, will need to be fed a carnivorous diet of live feed and commercial turtle pellets once each day. Requiring protein for their physical development, commercial pellets – containing about 40 percent of your pet's daily protein requirement – will make up half their daily feed, with the other half split between different live feed and the odd vegetarian or leafy treat. Once they pass the age of 12 months, red-eared slider hatchlings – now juveniles or yearlings – can be transitioned to the adult herbivorous diet. Yearlings and adults, on the other hand, can be fed a largely herbivorous diet with commercial turtle pellets comprising 25 percent of the feed, and the rest split between plants, vegetables and some live feed for protein once every two days.

The frequency of your feed also matters to the cleanliness and upkeep of the tank; any extra food left to collect in the substrate will begin to decay and contaminate the surroundings. As a rule of thumb, most red-eared slider owners and breeders have found that the ideal portion of commercial feed per feeding is equal to the size of the turtle's head. Therefore, those red-eared terrapins with larger heads with get a bigger handful of pellets, while smaller turtles should ideally get a smaller portion. Do not underestimate the greediness of the turtle, however; you can best determine how much each individual chelonian will need per feeding simply by observing how much it eats in one session.

On some occasions, a lack of diversity in the feed offered, lowered temperatures in the tank and other factors may lead to your red-eared turtle refusing food for prolonged periods. If you may need to entice your chelonians to stimulate their appetite, you can use a piece of debris from the tank, such as a small twig or log instead of your fingers and hand tweezers, and place the food on it. Then, wave the debris close to the red-eared slider, forcing it chase after its feed, should you be queasy about handling live feed, you can soak prepared feed in some tuna oil or brine to enhance its flavour and make it appetising for the turtle.

Some owners prefer to move their pets to a separate environment for feeding and foraging. This setting is usually a stripped-down or replicated version of the main housing tank, built simply for feeding purposes. After they are done, the owners then transfer the pets back into their original setting. This practice is considered convenient for those who do not like to dirty the tank with leftover food debris and cause potential ailments among the pets.

Know, however, that is not a necessary practice. While a good precautionary measure to take against illness, you can also ensure the wellbeing of your pet by simply being disciplined in the upkeep and cleanliness of your tank. Furthermore, shifting the red-eared sliders from one tank to another constantly may agitate them, cause them unnecessary stress and may even injure them in the process.

As long as you remember to clear away fecal matter and food debris a few hours after every feed, and filter and change the water on a regular basis, your environment should be healthy enough to house your Slider Turtles for feeding as well as basking and rest. It is preferable that you feed the terrapins during the day, in order to complement their feeding routines in the wild. It is also essential that you maintain a regular frequency of enhancing your pets' feed with the necessary nutritional supplements.

4. The Importance of freshness

One factor that ensures the health and well-being of your pets and cannot be compromised is the freshness of your feed. Old or stale feed is susceptible to fungal growth and mould that may make your red-eared sliders very ill. Furthermore, mold can grow on just about any type of food - from the fresh produce you set aside as food treats to commercially-prepared food packages.

The best way to ensure fresh feed for your red-eared terrapins is to find a trusted brand sold by reliable outlets and vendors, and stick with them. Before every purchase, take the time to check if the bags are sealed and the food has been recently manufactured. If you find that the pellets are on sale and the price has been steeply reduced, pay close attention to the expiry date and contents. Some vendors may try to lure customers into buying older stock at lower prices to clear their shelves faster.

You may also be attracted to larger turtle pellet tins and bags that are economical and provide greater "value for money". Before you make your purchase, understand that all types of food become vulnerable to moldy growth almost as soon as it has been opened. Larger bags of food are a smart choice if you have a big group of turtles to care for, but may not be best for a single or pair of chelonians.

Optimum storage conditions also help to keep your feed fresh for longer. Most turtle pellets come in tins that, in itself may be a good short-term storage option, but if the feed is supposed to last you a long time, transfer the contents into airtight containers, preferably marked with the expiry dates.

Every few weeks, take an inventory of the feed you have stored aside. If expired food is harmful to your health, it is equally bad for your red-eared slider turtles. Do not feed them any food that has spoiled, collected mold or its past its shelf-life; any interaction with toxic substances can be fatal to their life.

5. What not to feed your Red-eared Slider Turtle

Once you settle into a feeding pattern with your red-eared slider turtle, you may find that their palates can be easy to please; all they require is a constant supply of commercially-manufactured feed to keep them satiated, supplemented by a small portion of plant life and some type of live feed. Such a healthy appetite may cause some to believe that these chelonians can be fed almost any type of food; this, however, is far from the truth. If you want to avoid health hazards among your tank members, ensure that your terrapins stay away from the following foods:

1.   Bread is not only a source of minimal nutrition to us, but also to red-eared slider turtles. Composed mainly of empty calories and sugar, these pets have a weakness for bread, and will ignore any nutritious food in its presence. Copious amounts of bread will fatten up your turtle without providing them with any useful nutrition. In their excitement, your pet may also try to swallow too much dry bread, which could lead to choking hazards.

2.   Many fruits may be too sugar-laden for your red-eared slider turtle on a daily basis, and cause digestive issues. Citric fruits such as oranges, lemons, grapefruit, and others like banana and apples are best fed as rare treats to your turtle.

3.   Other fresh produce that may be healthy for you but is incredibly toxic for chelonians includes leafy greens and produce with high oxalic acid, such as spinach. These foods may inhibit absorption of calcium by the body, leading to Metabolic Bone Disease (MBD).

4.   Chocolate is also known to be highly toxic for red-eared sliders and can lead to poisoning, convulsions, nervous disorders, and death.

5.   Processed foods that are high in salts, sugar and unhealthy fats are just as bad for your pets as they are for you. While they may not be toxic for the pet, even tiny portions of processed foods may be too fatty for them.

6.   Fatty foods in general are best kept away from your red-eared slider. Along with avocados and fatty processed foods, nuts should also be avoided. Along with filling your red-eared slider turtle with fatty content they don't require, nuts also may become trapped in the red-eared slider turtle's bills and choke them.

6. Toxicity through Flora and Feed

While we can collect considerable information on the health effects that common plants, live feed, fruits and vegetables have on red-eared slider health, we still haven't completely understood which plants bring about toxic reactions. Based on their ability to adapt to varying semi-aquatic conditions in the environment, it can be assumed that these chelonians are immune to the toxic effects in at least several, if not all locally growing flora.

Therefore, while your pet may not be able to accurately reveal toxic vegetation in your area, you should take the time to inspect the plant life that your red-eared terrapins will be housed in. Even if the pets themselves avoid being poisoned, you could easily come into contact with these plants while handling your pets.

You can also speak to the local flora and exotic pet or chelonian experts to discover what local plants may be harmful to your red-eared slider, if any. Familiarize yourself with common plant-life in your region to help avoid any accidental mishaps among your pets.

Toxicity may also be caused through poisonous substances that have been ingested from the terrapin's immediate surroundings. If the red-eared slider turtle chances upon feed infected with bacteria, they may contract one of many forms of food poisoning that cause weakness, paralysis and death. Other mould and toxic growths may result in such health defects as respiratory infections, organ haemorrhage, and liver damage. To help keep your pet safe from unnecessary toxicity, it is best to keep its feed constantly refreshed past the sell-by date, and stored in dry and airtight conditions at all times.

Chapter 7: Caring for your Red-eared Slider Turtle

1. Handling your Red-eared Slider Turtle

It doesn't matter if you've been holding your terrapin since the day it was born; as hatchlings, red-eared slider turtles may be too delicate to handle for prolonged periods, and as adults, will discourage you from holding them as much as they can. You may wisely want to give your chelonian their freedom and not hold them too often, but certain circumstances will require you to lift, hold and even examine the reptiles for injuries and ailments.

You may be as stealthy and quiet as a whisper, and still find it next to impossible to successfully handle your red-eared terrapin - don't be disheartened. Red-eared sliders are slippery, surprisingly strong and precocious reptiles who take great pride in their ability to evade capture. In such situations, it is smart to replicate the calm demeanour displayed by your reptile and its settings. Any sudden movements, noise or a large group of people will agitate the pet and cause it to react defensively, by hissing, scratching at you, swimming rapidly away or even emptying their bowels as a sign of aggression. The best way to handle your pet is to approach it stealthily when it is basking.

Lifting your red-eared slider turtle

Once you do manage to approach your red-eared slider, lifting them the right way is of utmost importance. Remember, an adult turtle is significantly larger, heavier and more aggressive than a young one, so its defence tactics are likely to hurt you more. Another point to remember is that red-eared slider turtle cannot and should not be lifted in the same casual way as other domestic animals, such as dogs or cats. Do not attempt to lift them by their feet as they are strong and will kick out at you; you may cause them severe injury, possibly even a fracture.

The smartest way to lift your red-eared slider is to enclose the body from the sides with your hands in a calm and slow movement. When you lift the reptile, its limbs should tuck in neatly and firmly against its body to prevent it from kicking at you, either in fight or fright. As your pet has sharply-tipped feet, you will also need support them by placing a hand beneath its feet. This clasp also prevents the chelonian from clawing at you with its nails.

Once you have finished examining your pet, place it back down as calmly and gently as you can. Sudden and quick movements may cause the reptile to become agitated and even result in injuries as they are released. Understand that most red-eared sliders in general, and some individual pets, in particular, may not want to be handled unless absolutely necessary; too much pressure may not only agitate them, but also cause duress to their physical frame.

Interacting with Red-eared sliders and the risk of Salmonella

Since the risk of exposure to salmonella from red-eared slider turtles is easily avoided through proper sanitary practices, it is best to practice safe handling techniques, and educate others on the same. In spaces that house several types of pets together, red-eared slider turtles should be kept separate from such species as chickens, who are ready carriers of bacterial parasites.

1. Reserve a pair of clothing and shoes specifically for red-eared slider handling purposes. Ensure that these clothes and shoes are cleaned and disinfected after interaction with your pets. Avoid letting your turtles roam in such areas as the kitchen, bathroom or any space in your living quarters that contains food or clothing meant for human consumption.

2. Remember to wash your hands and face after each visit to the tank, and supervise younger children during their cleanliness rituals. Ensure that such activities as handling, feeding cleaning and egg hatching are undertaken by as few people as possible; introducing the turtles to several

humans at once – especially children - increases the risk of spread of infection among all involved parties.

3. Finally, play your part towards educating children and other adults in the rights methods to interact with and care for red-eared slider turtles.

2. Transporting your Red-eared Slider Turtle

Content though they may be within their tank, you will face many instances during which you may have to transport your red-eared sliders to other locations. These may include trips to the local pet expert, or even longer journeys that may require boarding an airplane. Whatever be the circumstance, transporting your chelonian comfortably – and legally – is an issue of importance, as they are easily stressed, require stabilized conditions and can also cause both, a mess and a stench in your vehicle. Among the most preferred containers through which to drive your red-eared slider around are:

Plastic and Cardboard Containers

Plastic or cardboard containers are the cheapest, and also the simplest means through which you can comfortably cart your pet around. Your entire transportation tub requires a short-enough height with a firm roof that prevents the pet from climbing out when startled. You then drill a few well-placed holes into the roof and the side walls, as a means to facilitate air flow in the tub. Make the floor comfortable and hygienic for the reptile by layering the bottom surface with piles of towels and newspapers shavings; it will also absorb and hold any food or waste material produced by your pet, along with offering burrowing possibilities. Remember that red-eared sliders should never be transported in an aquatic setting – this may cause unnecessary mishaps, injuries, even drowning.

The only factor to keep in mind is that your red-eared slider should be as stress-free as possible. Since their stress is often caused by unfamiliar sights or sounds, especially if they are easily frightened, try and provide opaque transportation tubs for your transportation needs. These will shield your pets away from the outside world, while the dark colours and environment will help them relax and encourage burrowing. If you must use translucent or transparent-toned plastic tubs, try and cover them with a light cloth to provide some obstacle.

It is also essential that you maintain a regulated temperature within the transportation box in order to keep the pet as calm as possible. A comfortable setting between 75-80 degrees Fahrenheit should help encourage digging and sleeping in your pet while in motion.

Tips to ensure safe red-eared slider turtle transportation

1. Secure your transportation container to your vehicle to prevent it from sliding around and causing either stress or a mess. You can do this by buckling the seat belt around the container, or even use heavy-duty straps or bungee cords. This safety measure will ensure that your red-eared slider is not thrown around the vehicle in case of turbulence.

2. Some people feel that the odour caused by turtles housed in a small space for long periods of time can become overwhelming during transportation, even causing nausea. Should you find yourself in a similar position, understand that it is perfectly safe to transport your pet in the cargo or exterior storage section of your vehicle; ensure that the tub or cage is firmly attached secured to your vehicle.

3. If the temperatures in your surroundings fall below the recommended maximum of 75 degrees Fahrenheit, you can provide heat with a hot-water bottle. Wrap the bottle in a sock or a towel and place within the box in a corner. You can also place the wrapped bottle inside a small resealable plastic bag for additional safety.

4. If the temperatures in your surroundings exceed the recommended maximum of 80 degrees Fahrenheit, you can cool your pet using a water spray or cool cloth. Place the container

away from direct sunlight, and try to adjust the temperature with your air-conditioner.

5. Try to avoid transporting your pet with a large group of people, as the noise and crowd may be unsettling for the pets. Loud music and other disturbing behaviour may also cause stress, making the cargo section ideal for peaceful transportation.

6. If you are transporting your red-eared slider over long distances and need to board an airplane, consult with your airline to learn the necessary transportation and medical precautions that need to be undertaken.

7. Remember to ask about and complete such air transport procedures as filing the necessary paperwork, ensuring that your pet has received the necessary vaccinations and clearances, and securing permits for transport in the passenger cabin.

8. Finally, ensure that all travelling companions – whether your fellow car passengers, or crew and staff aboard your airline – are aware of the presence of your pet and are comfortable with having the pet stowed around them or under your seat (in case of air travel).

3. Caring for your Red-eared Slider Turtle in the winter

The winter months are a crucial time in the life cycle of a red-eared slider turtle, whether in captivity or in the wild. In the wild, most red-eared terrapins survive the winter season by entering a state of partial hibernation – known as brumation – while nestled safely at the depth of such freshwater bodies as ponds. It is the thick vegetative flooring at the bottom, along with the densely muddy embankments that provide red-eared sliders with the necessary protection needed to survive the months.

During this brumative period, red-eared sliders experience very low levels of activity, owing to the lower consumption yet higher burning rate of oxygen at colder temperatures. This partial shutdown is also helped by the red-eared slider turtle's ability to absorb oxygen from its surroundings through the membranes around its throat, mouth and even cloaca. Mostly undertaken in order to survive the bitter chill in most North American states, this state of torpor pauses such daily activities as basking, feeding and even swimming, until the conditions above water are favourable once more.

In theory, to help your pets survive the winter months, brumation should be necessary particularly if you live in areas that experience bitter winters (such as parts of the United States and Canada). Through a prolonged period spent in captivity across diverse geographical borders, however, it has been found red-eared slider turtles can actually spend the winter months without the needing to brumate, if given the right climatic and aquatic settings. An intricately complicated life process, a red-eared slider turtle that does enter a state of brumation in captivity may not always find conditions favourable enough to get out of the state. Furthermore, the aquatic set-up provided by a captive environment may not have a depth or surface area favorable enough for successful brumation. Irregularities in the water temperature may cause the turtles to enter a state of shock. An inability on your part to maintain the right temperature of the water at all times could send your pet to a slow drowning death (if the water is too cold).

Whether your chelonians are housed outdoors, or raised inside your home also impacts the personal decision to enter a hibernated state. It is never easy to accurately isolate the factors and causes that successfully take red-eared sliders in and out of the brumative state. As an amateur pet owner, you may have a rough idea of the ideal water temperature and lighting settings for effective brumation, but unless you can replicate the red-eared slider's natural habitat in captivity for the winter months, and have sufficient experience in doing so, keeping your terrapins awake during the winter is the best course of action. You will also need to monitor your pet's' progress every few days, without disturbing their state of torpor. Any deviation from the routine may only serve to stress your pet through the winter months instead of helping it thrive.

As a caregiver, therefore, you will have to take the time to determine whether you truly want to encourage brumation in your turtles. You will then need to assess your housing set-up for its readiness to protect your red-eared sliders against the harsh cold. Regardless of the care they can offer and their geographical location, professional red-eared slider breeders and pet owners most often make the decision to discourage brumation and keep their turtles active in the winter.

Setting the tank up for winter

An outdoor housing set-up may expose the red-eared terrapins to chilly drafts of wind during the winter, and must be immediately switched for indoor housing. If you are unable to move your slider indoor due to space or time constraints, you will then need to ensure that the housing areas are enclosed within a wind-proof insulated covering. It's best to prepare in advance by isolating a room on your premises - such as an empty bedroom, tool shed or garage - that can be left undisturbed by members in your house.

For an aquatic set-up that discourages brumation, set the water temperature between 75-78 F (24-26 C), ensuring that it does not dip to lower temperatures abruptly. In the wild, red-eared sliders combat the winter months by avoiding food during the brumative state. In captivity, you will continue to feed them as per your regular schedule, taking special care to monitor your pet's appetite. Water that is cold may shut down hunger responses in the turtles, yet if it isn't cold enough may not kick start the brumative process, placing your pet in a state of limbo. If left unchecked, this avoidable mishap could spell the end of your turtle.

You may also lose out on hours of natural light in an indoor housing set-up during winter, so ensure that you have the necessary UVA and UVB lighting fixtures in place to facilitate daily basking activity. Nothing can shut a red-eared slider's body down faster than an absence of heat and light; maintain a steady minimum of 12 hours of light each day to help keep your pets active and out of brumation.

4. Locating your missing your Red-eared Slider Turtle

Situation	Immediate Action	Long-term Action	Preventative Measures
Turtles lost within house	Lock all doors, windows, gates. Limit family members and pets to one room. Check all rooms, doorways, under surfaces. Check different floors within house. Check nooks/crannies/corners. Listen for faint scratching sound of claws against hard floors/walls.	Determine 1-2 week survival period in the wild. Set out bowl with water/food for turtle to find. Spend daytime hours searching for pet instead of night.	Set up better lids/screens for tank or housing enclosure. Set up preventive barriers at entry/exit of the house. Restrict free-range roaming. Invest in electronic tagging.
Turtles lost outside the house	Lock up all doors, windows, gates. Limit family members/ pets to one room. Check all rooms, doorways, adjoining interiors. Check areas that provide cover such as bushes/muddy banks. Check outdoor nooks/crannies/corners. Follow direction of local stream/pond or freshwater body if present nearby. Inspect community water bodies for	Determine 1-2 week survival period in the wild. Set out bowl with water/food for turtle to find. Spend daytime hours searching for pet instead of night. Enlist help of friends/family/local police/vet office/social media.	Set up better lids/screens for tank or housing enclosure. Set up preventive barriers at entry/exit of the property. Restrict free-range roaming. Invest in electronic tagging. Invest in such security measures as guard dog/electronic alarms

Situation	Immediate Action	Long-term Action	Preventative Measures
	potential basking zones. Listen for scratching sounds in areas with leafy, wood floor cover.		
Lost and found turtle	Inspect shell/limbs, skin for injury, cuts, wounds, abscess, physical trauma. Inspect bones and shell for fracture or bleeding. Check eyes, ears, appetite. Soak turtle in bowl of lukewarm water to clean away dirt/dust. Resume feeding as per normal/resist overfeeding.	Refer to veterinary hospital in case of any visible trauma symptoms. Isolate pet from other tank mates during the recovery period. Conduct round of laboratory tests to check for other possible ailments/injuries. Provide hydration by soaking turtle in Pedialyite solution as per instructions	Set up better lids/screens for tank or housing enclosure. Set up preventive barriers at entry/exit of the property. Restrict free-range roaming. Invest in electronic tagging. Invest in such security measures as guard dog/electronic alarms.

5.Entrusting others with your Red-eared Slider Turtle

Type of Care	Short-term care in your absence (under 48 hours)	Long-term care in your absence (over 48 hours)	Temporary care by another person	Re-homing red-eared sliders
Possible caregiver	Family member, friend, neighbor	Family member, friend, neighbor, house sitter	Family member, friend, neighbor, veterinary services,	Family member, friend, neighbors, hobbyists, rescue centres, breeders
Food	Will last up to 48 without needing another feed (adult) Provide instructions on live feed, vegetation, harmful foods Provide commercial feed to caregiver (if needed)	Add aquatic plants/feeder fish to sustain hunger Provide commercial feed to caregiver Provide instructions on live feed, vegetation, harmful foods	Add aquatic plants/feeder fish to sustain hunger Provide commercial feed to caregiver Provide instructions on live feed, vegetation, harmful foods	Provide/recommend preferred commercial feed and aquatic vegetation to caregiver Provide instructions on live feed, vegetation, harmful foods

Type of Care	Short-term care in your absence (under 48 hours)	Long-term care in your absence (over 48 hours)	Temporary care by another person	Re-homing red-eared sliders
Lighting	Set lighting periods with timer in system. Instruct caregiver to monitor lights/basking	Set lighting periods with timer in system Instruct caregiver to monitor lights/basking every 2-3 days	Set lighting periods with timer in system Instruct caregiver to monitor lights/basking every 2-3 days Provide replacement UVA/UVB bulbs	Recommend preferred lighting periods Instruct caregiver to monitor lights/basking every 2-3 days Recommend preferred UVA/UVB bulbs

Type of Care	Short-term care in your absence (under 48 hours)	Long-term care in your absence (over 48 hours)	Temporary care by another person	Re-homing red-eared sliders
Heat	Set predetermined regulated temperature with timer

Provide instructions on adjusting temperature

Instruct caregiver to monitor temperature | Set predetermined regulated temperature with timer

Provide instructions on adjusting temperature

Instruct caregiver to monitor temperature | Set predetermined regulated temperature with timer

Provide instructions on adjusting temperature

Instruct caregiver to monitor temperature

Provide replacement heating lamps/ thermometers | Provide instructions/ suggestions on proper temperature/ heat/basking conditions

Recommend preferred temperatures to caregiver

Provide/sugges t preferred heating lamps/ thermometers |
| Water | Filter once daily

Maintain regulated temperature | Filter once daily

Collect debris every 2 days

Maintain regulated temperature | Filter once daily

Collect debris every 2 days

Change water every 30 days

Disinfect and condition water | Provide instructions/su ggestions on proper water conditions

Recommend preferred water filters |

Type of Care	Short-term care in your absence (under 48 hours)	Long-term care in your absence (over 48 hours)	Temporary care by another person	Re-homing red-eared sliders
			Maintain regulated temperature	
Health/Safety	Ensure that turtle displays signs of health Predator and escape proof surrounding Provide handling instructions	Provide first-aid medication, pet expert contacts Instruct on basic first-aid, provide care sheet Predator and escape proof surrounding Provide handling instructions	Provide handling instructions Provide first-aid medication, pet expert contacts Instruct on basic first-aid, provide care sheet Recommend predator and escape proofing surroundings	Provide/ Recommend first-aid medication, pet expert contacts Instruct on basic first-aid, provide care sheet Recommend predator and escape proofing surroundings Provide handling instructions

Chapter 8: Health concerns for your Red-eared Slider Turtle

Red-eared slider turtles are among the more stronger of the reptilian creatures and have immune systems that can withstand most forms of illnesses and infection. They, however, are not infallible, and will become ill and infected if housed in extremely unhygienic conditions. Furthermore, most health-related ailments in red-eared slider turtles are of a nature that can only be isolated and diagnosed through laboratory examinations.

If provided with the right care, timely check-ups and a hygienic housing environment, most red-eared sliders will live their days in robust health, only affected in their old age by such ailments as shell-related decay or injuries, organ failure or drowning. Most common infections and physical ailment caused in these terrapins can be traced to an imbalance in their diet, poor housing conditions or external psychological factors that indirectly impact their emotional well-being.

A healthy red-eared slider turtle is alert even while basking and napping, and maintains a constant stream of activity such as swimming, foraging or basking throughout its waking hours. Red-eared sliders with no signs of infection or illness will have clear eyes, with no discharge oozing from the nose or ears. A smooth carapace with even and vibrant coloring and without any patches white growth, pinkish-red underlying hue or smell are other signs of a healthy red-eared slider; a cracked shell, injured limbs closed eyes and bleeding either from the shell or cloaca, are often indicators of a larger physical irregularity. Not prone to laziness, any displays of lethargic behaviour by your red-eared slider should cause concern, especially if accompanied by other red flags.

At the first sign of ill health, it is best to check that your red-eared slider is in no danger of drowning or dehydration. As a first-aid measure, you should try to raise the existing temperature of the tank (already set to 75 degrees Fahrenheit) by about 5 or 10 degrees Fahrenheit. This warmer setting should help your pet regulate its body temperature and activate bodily functions; most signs of listlessness or lethargy can be cured in this manner. Should this setting make no difference to the health of your pet, or if it becomes further distressed, rush your red-eared slider to the exotic pet expert for an immediate diagnosis.

If diagnosed with fatal illnesses past the initial stage of treatment, most red-eared sliders, despite their hardy and robust natures, are too far removed from their native settings to withstand the physical and emotional trauma that disease or injury may bring. In order to avoid such mishaps from breeding illness among your tank and putting you at a loss, it is best to practice healthy housing, cleaning and feeding methods that keep sickness at bay.

1. Common infections and maladies

Metabolic Bone Disease

Metabolic Bone Disease is a common ailment caused among those red-eared sliders in the development or adult stage who do not receive enough calcium and disproportionately large amounts of phosphorus in their diet. If left untreated, Metabolic Bone Disease, also known as MBD may lead to weakening of bones, contracting of other illnesses, and ultimately death.

An imbalance in the levels of calcium and phosphorus generally occurs when the red-eared slider's diet is rich in phosphorus, but not in calcium. A low supply of vitamin D3, essential for the absorption of calcium from food sources and provided by UVB rays, may also be a contributing factor. If housed indoors with little or no exposure to sunlight and inadequate basking facilities, red-eared sliders rely solely on food for their supply of this vitamin. If given in small amounts, their system may be unable to break down calcium, even if it is supplied in healthy doses. Food rich in oxalic acids such as spinach may further obstruct the absorption of calcium, further weakening your pet.

Once affected, the symptoms and effects of MBD can take weeks, even months of medication and rehabilitation to reverse, making prevention more essential that cure. Common symptoms include increased periods of drowsiness and lethargy, decreased activity and willingness to swim, bask, or walk, unsteady gait and movement, loss of appetite, noticeable frailty in bones, deformed physical appearance, possible bouts of seizures, and partial or complete paralysis. When handled, terrapins with MBD may also be extremely cool to the touch at all times - this is because MBD distorts the animal's ability to regulate body temperature, furthering weakening its health.

Attempts at warming up the reptile on your part may take longer than usual, and may exhaust the pet. Red-eared sliders should be taken to the veterinarian as soon as any symptoms of MBD are displayed. Depending on the severity of the condition, most pet experts will recommend a prolonged treatment with a calcium supplement, Rep Cal or similar. If your red-eared slider has already had seizures and may be on the verge of physical collapse or death, the veterinarian may even inject a direct dose of liquid calcium into the animal, to help it survive therapy and treatment.

Rep Cal and other calcium supplements will have to be added to each feed in the recommended doses; the pet will also have to be isolated from other tank mates, and kept in highly regulated conditions, due to its inability to regulate body temperature. Heating and lighting fixtures need to be adjusted to the right levels to promote quicker recovery.

Despite early signs of recovery, those terrapins who have had seizures during their encounter with MBD may still experience a fit once a week or less frequently for the next few months. It is best to monitor its health with the assistance of your local pet expert, to help ascertain that the chelonians recovery is on the right track. If attended to immediately and given the right kind of rehabilitation, red-eared slider turtles can make a recovery from MBD in a span of four weeks or even less.

Respiratory Infections

Respiratory Infections (RIs) are not only just as lethal to a red-eared terrapins health, if not more than, as MBD, but are also highly contagious and will also affect the health of other chelonians in the community housing. Not caused by one sole group of virus, RIs can arise from the reptile being exposed to a variety of inhospitable housing conditions, such as unhygienic and unfiltered water, a sudden prolonged exposure to cold drafts from outside the housing area, collection of food and fecal matter around the tank, an infection contracted from another tank mate, or even from accumulation of mold in their habitat that has not be cleaned away.

When affected, red-eared slider turtles will display such symptoms as exaggerated difficulty while breathing, accompanied by peculiar movements, known as listing. Listing is best defined as a series of swimming movement that are far removed from the turtle's normal swimming patterns. Undertaken through such acts as imbalanced movements, choppy manoeuvring and swimming in circles, this erratic series of activities occurs due to the build-up of fluid in the terrapin's lungs, which, when in tandem with uneven breathing patterns could be indicative of a larger underlying respiratory infection, possibly signalling pneumonia. Other symptoms exhibited by a red-eared slider affected with an RI include the following irregularities:

Respiratory Ailment	Normal Occurence	Cause for concern
Wheezing	During periods of high activity	Prolonged
Open mouth whilst breathing	Basking	Prolonged, accompanied by wheezing and discharge of mucus
Sneezing	Underwater	Prolonged in and out of water, mucus, wheezing, coughing
Coughing (with	Feeding	Prolonged and regular,

Respiratory Ailment	Normal Occurence	Cause for concern
or without vomit)		mouth rot
Yawning	Basking or underwater	Prolonged, wheezing, open mouth, lethargy, mucus
Bubbles from nose and mouth	Underwater	Prolonged, foamy discharge

Since RIs are often caused by unfavourable conditions in the chelonians environment, there are few medications that can directly help cure your pet. A veterinarian may be able to help alleviate discomfort and restore some lost health in the reptile by prescribing a treatment with an antibiotic known as Baytril. Like most other exotics, red-eared sliders often respond positively to Baytril and will likely seem to have made a recovery almost overnight - it is best to continue the treatment following the veterinarian's orders to prevent a possible relapse.

Those red-eared sliders who have been affected with RIs will need to be separated from their tank mates, and only returned when their recovery is complete and housing conditions in their original set-up are favourable. If the culprit behind the infection is an element within the tank, such as unfiltered water, unhygienic substrate or unregulated heating and lighting, other turtles will also have to be evacuated while the premises is disinfected and the flooring changed. Clothes worn during the disinfection process should also either be discarded or cleaned separately from other clothing; while red-eared sliders may not be able to pass on colds to you, viral strains from their infections could easily be transmitted to other susceptible organisms through such surfaces as clothing.

2. Shell-related issues:

Condition	Symptoms	Probable cause	Treatment
Algae growth	Pale green patches of algae growth appearing at sporadic intervals on the scutes	Mostly observed in outdoor aquatic housing facilities and wild red-eared sliders, not hazardous to health in small quantities	Gentle wiping of shell with soft moist cloth or soft-bristled toothbrush and water, filtration of water
Cracks/ Shell damage	Crack or hole in the scute, missing scute, foul smell, bleeding, infection, shock	Injury, attack, underlying infection or shell rot, with long-term exposure and neglected treatment leading to organ failure, disability, even death	First-aid in case of superficial shell damage; immediate medical attention in case of severe or persistent damage
Discoloration	Light or whitish patches on shell surface, golden appearance of certain scutes	Bacterial or fungal infection, mineral deposits or scutes shedding	Move turtle into sanitary conditions, monitor diet, water and filtration procedures, refer to pet expert in case of persistent discoloration
Unnatural coloring	Pink to red coloring around scutes, carapace,	Blood poisoning (septicaemia), caused due to previous injury,	Refer turtle to exotic pet veterinarian immediately

Condition	Symptoms	Probable cause	Treatment
	plastron, skin	illness, unsanitary conditions	
Fungal Growth	White to brown fuzzy clumps of growth on shell surface	Insufficient filtration of water, inadequate basking requirements, contracted from other infected turtles	Administer Repti Turtle Sulfa Dip for mild cases and external infections; report persistent cases to veterinarian
Mineral Deposit	Collection of white, chalky calcium and magnesium deposits on shell surface	Long-term exposure to hard water, while not hazardous to health, may affect structure and health of shell	Use filtered and purified water, preferably also de-chlorinated
Pyramid Syndrome	Rough appearance of shell, "pyramid" formations of scutes, uneven shell surface	Excess intake of fats and protein, leading to accelerated scute growth and uneven "pyramid" appearance, long-term exposure can lead to kidney failure and damaged shell	Reduce protein intake in food, monitor feeding, avoid overfeeding

Red-eared sliders and the Scute Shedding Phenomenon

The scutes on a red-eared slider turtle's shell function in a manner similar to the hair on human skin or the fur on mammalian bodies. Appendages that are comprised mainly of a protein compound called keratin, scutes are inherently "dead" by nature and extend outward from the turtle's body as a means of protection and adornment, with the oldest scutes found on the outermost parts of the shell.

Part of a continuous cycle of growth, shedding and re-emergence, the scutes on a red-eared slider's body shed and fall off to make way for new, healthy scutes, just as human or mammalian hair would. As old scutes separate from the shell, they allow pockets of air to nest between the shell and skin, lending the shell a golden hue. Accompanied by a subtle yet continuous lifting away from the skin, the light scutes eventually crack away from the turtle's body, making way for smoother, healthier scutes underneath.

The shedding period among our red-eared slider friends, however, is not always a subtle or consistent process, and may be startling to the untrained eye. The frequency and intervals between shedding periods varies greatly from one red-eared slider to another, and is largely reliant on such factors as the amount of time devoted to basking, dietary and housing conditions. As an amateur turtle owner, you may have witnessed an abrupt "breakage" of either small bits or large pieces of scutes from your pets, with shell casings scattered across the tank. Do not be worried; this process, that occurs once or even twice a year among certain turtles, is known as scute shedding.

As the owner, there is little, if anything, that can be done to accelerate the scute shedding process in your turtle. This natural phenomenon may sometimes take a week to achieve completion; some red-eared sliders, however, seem to shed for months at a time – understand that either pattern of shedding is normal and should not arouse concern. So long as the scutes underneath have a smooth appearance and developing color, scute shedding is a relatively incident-free process that should not be confused with shell-related damage to the turtle.

It is a combination of optimum basking time during the day, adequate minerals and vitamins for shell growth and a suitable housing environment that encourage scute shedding. Providing the requisite factors, and then allowing you turtle to dismiss of its old scutes is perhaps the wisest way to promote new scute growth without disturbing the pet's health or temperament.

3. Digestive ailments

Ailment	Symptoms	Probable cause	Treatment
Vomiting/ Hacking cough	Throwing out food particles and blood through persistent cough and vomit	Obstruction of food passages by large pieces of food, pieces of gravel from substrate Prolonged cough/vomiting may suggest underlying RI	Refer to pet expert for immediate treatment Collect sample of vomit/discharge for testing Isolate pet from tank mates until recovery
Constipation	No signs of waste collected at the bottom of the tank Sudden loss of appetite	Inadequate fibre content in diet Obstruction of internal passages due to ingested pebbles, gravel from substrate Cold temperatures leading to overall lethargy and inactivity	Place turtle in water measuring around 78 degrees Fahrenheit (32-35 degrees Celsius) for thirty minutes to help stimulate activity

Ailment	Symptoms	Probable cause	Treatment
			Ask pet expert for X-ray in case of swallowed objects Remove all objects from tank with potential to be ingested Increase fibre content in pet's diet
Irregular stool	Runny, liquid appearance, deviation from hard, green to brown colored appearance, presence of blood in stool	Disproportionate fibre, mineral, vitamin content, appearance of blood may suggest impaction as well	Ask pet expert for laboratory test of provided stool sample Remove all objects from tank with potential to be ingested Review and regulate content in pet's diet
Internal parasites	Presence of worms or similar parasites in stool	Unhygienic housing conditions, contracted from open injury, other turtles, or from parasites in live feed	Immediate laboratory sample of stool, quarantine from other turtles until full recovery is made

Ailment	Symptoms	Probable cause	Treatment
Blood from Cloaca	Direct bleeding through the cloaca, or presence of blood in stool	May be caused due to impaction of excretory passages	Ask pet expert for X-ray in case of swallowed objects Remove all objects from tank with potential to be ingested Increase fibre content in pet's diet
Aversion toward eating	Abrupt loss of appetite, dull/listless behaviour, refusal to accept feed, lowered rate of activity, signs of brumation	Dependence on yolk sac immediately after hatching, decreased metabolism owing to low temperatures, monotony in diet, readiness for egg-laying, stress and trauma from previous injury/illness, underlying illness	Maintain consistent temperature of 75-78 degrees Fahrenheit (32-35 degrees Celsius), introduce new foods into diet, try enticing practices, separate pet from tank mates (in case of aversion to food caused by bullying incidents)

4. Other possible ailments

Ailment	Symptoms	Probable cause	Treatment
Injury/ infection of eye	Partially/complete ly shut/swollen eyes, rubbing of eyes after changing of water	Caused by poor housing and hygienic conditions, dehydration, deficiency of Vitamin A, underlying RI, trauma from physical injury, excessive chlorine levels in water	Treat swollen or shut eyes as immediate sign of underlying illness or trauma Request for X-rays and laboratory tests to check for RI and other ailments Increase dosage of Vitamin A drops or cod-liver oil around eye area (in absence of RI) Use de-chlorinated water and monitor levels Pet must be isolated from

Ailment	Symptoms	Probable cause	Treatment
			other tank mates during recovery
Abscess in ear	Visible lump on one or both sides of head, inflamed, tender appearance, partially/completely shut or swollen eyes, imbalanced swimming and other impaired motor functions	Caused by poor housing and hygienic conditions, dehydration, deficiency of Vitamin A, underlying RI, trauma from physical injury, excessive chlorine levels in water	Requires immediate draining of fluid from infection site, along with subsequent disinfection Difficult to treat without immediate veterinary assistance Pet must be isolated from other tank mates during recovery
Irregular appearance of nails	Overgrown or chipped nails, tender or sore around affected area, discharge from wound	Injury sustained during mating, fighting or digging gravel, infection caused due to poor housing and hygiene conditions	Pet must be isolated from other tank mates during treatment Place turtle in dry area and administer Neosporin or Nolvasan as needed

Ailment	Symptoms	Probable cause	Treatment
			Refer to pet expert for subsequent treatment
Stomatitis (Mouth rot)	Formation of ulcers around tongue, throat, inside and exterior of mouth area, white-yellow blisters around mouth, coughing accompanied by mucus, bleeding around mouth area	Bacterial or viral infection caused by poor housing and hygiene conditions, may prove lethal if left unchecked, and will be transmitted to other tank mates	Requires immediate treatment of ulcers infection site, along with subsequent disinfection Difficult to treat without immediate veterinary assistance Pet must be isolated from other tank mates during recovery
Intestinal/ Reproductive prolapse	Appearance of intestinal and/or reproductive organs from cloaca with inability to retract unaided	Temporary or prolonging intestinal/reproductive disorder, injury sustained during mating or fighting, egg binding (in females)	Requires immediate treatment of ulcers infection site, along with subsequent disinfection Difficult to treat without immediate veterinary

Ailment	Symptoms	Probable cause	Treatment
			assistance Pet must be isolated from other tank mates during recovery
Penile prolapse	Appearance of male penis from cloaca with inability to retract unaided	Temporary or prolonging reproductive disorder, injury sustained during mating, fighting or swallowing gravel	Pet must be isolated from other tank mates immediately Place turtle in water measuring around 78 degrees Fahrenheit for thirty minutes to help stimulate activity Refer to pet expert for immediate treatment

5. Red-eared Slider Turtles and behavioural issues

Aggression

- Causes:
    - o Inadequate space in basking zone
    - o Inadequate space within housing area
    - o Imbalanced number of males and females in tank
    - o Arrival of new tank mate
- Treatment:
    - o Provide ample completely dry space for basking
    - o Ensure privacy in case of new pets
    - o Observe dynamics with tank mates and isolate if necessary
    - o Provide necessary solitary nesting spaces for egg-laying females away from harassing males
    - o Provide separate feeding/basking timings if necessary

Not enough time spent basking

- Causes:
    - o Very warm temperatures of water that discourage basking,
    - o Excessively high/low temperature setting within housing area,
    - o Inadequate space in basking zone, absence of heat source, stressful dynamics between tank mates, insufficient privacy
- Treatment:
    - o Regulate temperature of water to 75-78 degrees Fahrenheit (24-25.5 degrees Celsius) and basking area to 90-95 degrees Fahrenheit (32.2-35 degrees Celsius)
    - o Provide ample completely dry space for basking Ensure privacy in case of new pets

Excessive time spent basking, general listlessness, lowered rate of activity, lethargic movements

- Causes:
    o Excessively cold temperatures of water and housing,
    o nervousness if newly acquired, bullying from other tank mates,
    o possible underlying respiratory infection
- Treatment:
    o Observe dynamics with tank mates and isolate if necessary
    o Increase water temperature to 75-78 degrees Fahrenheit (24-25.5 degrees Celsius)
    o Refer to pet expert for necessary tests and X-rays
    o Provide adequate privacy and conditions in case of new pet

Restless behaviour, agitated appearance and movements

- Causes:
    o Insufficient adjustment time (in case of new pet), inadequate temperature settings,
    o stress due to previous of underlying illness, readiness to lay eggs (in case of female),
    o incorrect handling from owner
- Treatment:
    o Regulate temperature of water to 75-78 degrees Fahrenheit (24-25.5 degrees Celsius) and basking area to 90-95 degrees Fahrenheit (32.2-35 degrees Celsius)
    o Observe dynamics with tank mates and isolate if necessary
    o Provide adequate privacy and conditions in case of new pet
    o Provide necessary nesting spaces for egg-laying females

Erratic movements, unnatural movements while swimming, walking, unbalanced gait, circular movements

- Causes:
    - o Fluid build up in lungs,
    - o respiratory infection,
    - o probable ear infection,
    - o inconsistent temperature settings within the tank, stressful dynamics between tank mates,
    - o insufficient privacy
- Treatment:
    - o Observe dynamics with tank mates and isolate if necessary
    - o Provide adequate privacy and conditions in case of new pet
    - o Regulate temperature of water to 75-78 degrees Fahrenheit (24-25.5 degrees Celsius)
    - o Check for probable ear or respiratory infections and provide necessary treatment

6. Treating common Red-eared Slider Turtle ailments

Treating superficial shell injuries:

When you first spot a crack or bump around the carapace or plastron area of your red-eared slider turtle, the best immediate response is to isolate your slider from its tank mates and closely inspect the terrapin for signs of bleeding. Fresh shell injuries will likely bleed to some extent, making the severity of the wound hard to determine until first aid is provided. To effectively treat a superficial bleeding injury in your red-eared slider:

● Place the turtle in a separate plastic storage container for temporary inspection and medication. If your turtle resists handling and treatment, you can avoid being bitten by placing a wad of soft towel or cloth in your pet's mouth.

• Use a thick, clean towel to press on the affected area, and apply slight pressure on the shell to contain the bleeding.

• Only once the bleeding has either reduced or stopped completely should you administer medication. Acceptable antibacterial soaps and wound disinfectants include Betadine and Hibiclens, easily found at most local pharmacies.

• Fill a large bowl with lukewarm water, lower your turtle into the bowl and use a clean brush with soft bristles to apply the disinfectant for your turtle. Hold your turtle down firmly as you scrub the affected area with the water and medicine.

• Then, transfer your pet back into the dry temporary storage area for about three to four hours, to allow the terrapin's injury to heal and repair. Repeat this process once daily until your red-eared slider's injury has healed completely.

• Apart from visible signs of bleeding under the shell, a serious injury to the carapace or plastron is also indicated by a rank, foul smell, an unnaturally soft shell texture or discoloration that deviates from the pet's regular markings. If the affected area exhibits any of these signs at any point before or during the first-aid process, it is best to rush your red-eared slider to the veterinarian.

• No matter how little the injury or cut is, it's best to monitor its healing on a daily basis, and contact your exotic pet expert in case the injury worsens or becomes infected.

Treating minor cuts, wounds and attacks from predators:

Apart from providing relief and medication for shell-related ailments, treatments for your red-eared slider turtle can also be directly administered to treat injuries like cuts and wounds caused due to injury, fights with tank mates or attack by predators. As with applying medication to the shell, it is essential that your red-eared slider is comfortable with your presence and is contained firmly within your grasp. If they react aggressively towards your advances and tactics to subdue them, it may only serve to aggravate their injuries. Here is a list of common predators for your red-eared slider turtle:

Predatory Terrain	Common Predators
Terrestrial	Snakes, foxes, dogs, wolves, coyotes, weasels, minks, bobcats, opossums, racoons, dingoes, skunk, rats, badgers, ferrets, cats, bears
Aerial	Hawks, falcons, owls, crows, ravens
Marine	Otters, herons, turtles, crocodiles, frogs, large fish

Treating red-eared sliders in case of drowning:

Though it may seem unlikely, red-eared slider turtles, like all other chelonians are susceptible to drowning, especially in a captive setting with inadequate housing facilities. Adept swimmers by nature, cases of drowning will often occur if a turtle has turned over while in water and does not have the required space to right itself.

In need of oxygen, many red-eared sliders will temporarily brumate, waiting for external assistance. Despite sinking to the bottom of the tank, they may still not have died, and can be resuscitated, if taken out of the water and provided with treatment Ensure that you provide immediate first-aid attention and make hasty preparation to seek veterinary help.

● Never attempt to place a drowning turtle on its back, as this may constrict the already-clogged airspace in its lungs and kill the pet.

● Hold your turtle's neck, clasping at the base of the skull behind the ears. Then, extend the neck as far as possible.

● Now, release excess water from the lungs by holding the turtle with its head facing downwards and tail facing upward. Ensure that your grip on the neck is secure throughout.

• Carefully place your turtle on its belly on a broad flat surface, still maintaining your grip around the neck.

• Standing in front of your turtle (facing its head), grasp and extend its front legs in your direction as far as possible.

• Now, holding its legs straight, pump them backwards into its chest, ensuring that you do not bend its limbs at the elbow joints. Repeat this back-and-forth pumping action to help the turtle cough out any remaining water.

• As soon as the excess water has been drained, rush your pet to your local veterinary hospital to begin such procedures as supplying of oxygen and a possible prescription of antibiotics (in case your turtle has contracted pneumonia in the process). Some owners have claimed to have success by encouraging straw-to-mouth breathing as a means of oxygen supply. This method, however, has not been verified for accuracy and is not a substitute for veterinary attention. It is the speed and accuracy of your actions that can help prevent drowning and save your turtle's life.

Knowing when to seek external medical assistance

Most illnesses and ailments that will affect your red-eared sliders will likely be caused by an imbalance in their diet, improper housing conditions or stress caused by external factors. As an invasive species, disposable though they may seemingly be, red-eared slider turtles in captivity still deserve protection against illnesses and infections owing to the difference between the conditions of captive environment and their natural habitat. While health care for this terrapin may require slightly more time than a dog or cat, the long-term health of your pet will benefit you as well.

In many cases, superficial shell wounds and bruises can be treated at home, without seeking medical assistance. As long as your red-eared slider is swimming, walking, feeding and basking well, is active and not displaying signs of if listlessness or stress, medical attention may need consist of no more than separating the pet from its tank mates for a two or three days and providing the right medication or behaviour therapy.

A minor cold or injury, should not greatly affect the behavior or daily routine of your terrapin in any drastic way. Red-eared sliders will only display erratic behavior and overt signs of physical discomfort when they have been affected by a serious underlying medical condition. Should your pet witness an abrupt shift in behavioral patterns or motor function, or suffer severe medical trauma, it becomes important to contact your veterinarian at the earliest.

If your red-eared slider turtle is in need of urgent expert medical attention, it will display such signs as:

● Blood from the cloaca,

● A seizure episode,

● Partial or complete paralysis,

● Sudden and constant discharge from the eyes or ears,

● Loss of or partial or complete limb or tail (due to injury).

Your terrapin may not always display signs that are physical manifestations of an underlying illness. In some cases, illnesses such as Metabolic Bone Disease and Respiratory infections may only hinted at by observing the reptile's movements and symptoms for 24-48 hours. If your chelonian displays the following signs for over 48 hours, it is best to rush it to your exotic pet expert at the earliest:

● Prolonged loss of appetite,

● Pink or red patches or spots under the shell surface,

● Abscesses around the ears,

● Refusal to eat or bask,

● Discharge from nose or eyes,

- Dull, listless behavior.

- Irregular and erratic swimming/movement patterns

In order to prepare your exotic pet expert to provide the right type of treatment, it is advisable that you call ahead and inform the medical staff of your red-eared slider's emergency. In cases of immediate surgery or drowning, such arrangements as oxygen supply and an operation room will have to be prepared in advance. This intimation also allows the medical staff to direct you to another pet expert, should your veterinarian not be present at the time. Collecting and carrying such samples as stool, vomit and shed skin or shell components will also help your veterinarian diagnose and treat your pet with speed and accuracy.

7. Preventing health concerns for your Red-eared Slider Turtle

If you are the type of pet owner who is attentive, considerate and dedicated, then you most likely will already have a care-giving system that is mindful of your red-eared slider's needs. In an ideal environment that gives the terrapin the right type of food, housing, basking, swimming and hygiene conditions, there is little chance that your pet will incur anything more serious than the odd fight-related injury or scruff to the shell.

Even so, it is always best to take every precaution necessary to safeguard your chelonian against the possibility of illness and disease. Not only are all diseases physically draining for the terrapin, but several infections sustained by these reptiles may also infect other tank mates. Here are a few ways by which you can ensure the health and well-being of your pet:

1. A daily inspection of your red-eared slider's water for food remains and excrement is not only preferable, it is also essential. As adults, these chelonians eat generously, shed equally copious amounts of excrement, and create a mess with that could quickly contaminate an enclosed space.

2. Any kind of food that could decay and compost, along with all the excrement, should be cleaned out once daily.

3. The water will be filtered for the most part with your installed systems, but will still need to be changed once every 30-45 days. The substrate and flooring within the housing, if provided, will also have to be replaced once every 4-6 months. This will avoid the possibility of any infestations from rotting matter.

4. It is best to avoid putting in such items as small, easy-to swallow stones, twigs, gravel and allergens such as sawdust into the cage. Since red-eared slider turtles are curious and slightly greedy creatures, they may try to eat objects they do not understand, leading to possible choking hazards and internal injuries.

5. Being cold-blooded by nature, red-eared slider turtles thrive best when housed in consistent temperatures and conditions that mimic their natural surroundings. They become easily stressed if the temperature within their housing is either susceptible to erratic shifts, or is beyond their adaptability range. As chelonians, a consistent water temperature of 75-78 degrees Fahrenheit (24-25.5 degrees Celsius) and basking area temperature of 90-95 degrees Fahrenheit (32.2-35 degrees Celsius) for adults, while maintaining the same in the winter months will keep your terrapins safe from the hazards of unexpected hibernation or stressful behavior.

6. Ensure that you provide a specific zone for basking activities, and equip it in a way that enhances your turtle's' health. Provide ample space for all tank mates, and ensure that the platform is as dry as possible. Supplement the basking zone with adequate heating and lighting fixtures, while ensuring the basking area is injury-and-escape-proof.

7. Keep a keen eye on the interaction of your red-eared sliders with other tank mates, members in your house and its immediate surroundings. These terrapins are expressive by nature and will display aggressive behaviors or visible signs of trauma when faced with injury or a perceived threat.

8. In case of newly acquired red-eared sliders in a community setting, provide between 60-90 days for the new terrapin in a

solitary tank or container. This allows the terrapin to acclimatize to its surroundings, lowers risks of being bullied by older members in the community and allows to ascertain the health of the new pet.

9. Finally, closely monitor your role as the primary source of food for the terrapins, along with the amount of food needed by your pets. Plan and prepare a diet that contains a healthy proportion of live feed, turtle pellets, aquatic plants and necessary vegetation, and ensure a steady supply of calcium, phosphorus, Vitamin D3 and other essential nutrients.

8. The importance of Veterinary care

Experienced and professional though they may be, veterinarians for animals such as cats, dogs, rabbits, hamsters etc. may not always be the best people to treat your cold-blooded pond-sliding reptilians. These poikilothermic creatures require special care from chelonian experts who have specialized in and are more familiar with the health requirements of red-eared slider turtles. The good news is, finding an exotic reptile pet health expert is an easy-enough process.

If you do not already have a veterinary expert to contact, your red-eared slider turtle sellers, retailers or breeders will all be happy to help you. Breeders and retailers usually have the best sources on call, since the health of their terrapins is their top priority. If these options don't work out for you, however, some simple research of your own will yield plenty of results.

Many experts offering exotic pet and reptilian health care services advertise on the Internet and can be located within a few minutes. Additionally, you can also rely on feedback and reviews from other breeders and owners to narrow down the best option for your red-eared sliders.

Once you find your exotic pet expert, it is best to take your pet up to them for an initial examination. To help avoid exposing your pets as to prolonged interaction with strangers or unhygienic conditions, and to provide faster treatment for your pet, try to find an expert who is willing to make house calls, especially if you own a larger group of ill turtles. Many experts understand the relative complications involved in transporting a large group of aquatic reptiles in a cramped vehicle, and are more than willing to oblige you.

9. Providing insurance for your Red-eared Slider Turtle

Animals such as red-eared slider turtles are referred to as exotics since they require exacting standards for housing, diet and health care in order to live a long life that is without any medical complications. Despite your best intentions, it may not always be able to provide the daily rigorous care that the sliders may require; it is difficult to tell exactly how many turtle pellets and live feed are right for their daily diet, or it may be difficult to replicate the conditions needed for successful brumation and basking.

It is perhaps because of reasons like these, that when red-eared slider turtles do succumb to illnesses, they are often of a recurring nature and require long-term care. A red-eared slider turtle who contracts a respiratory infection may have a weak immune system and may be constantly susceptible to infections; another pet with shell or digestive disorders may constantly need medical supervision and repeated rounds of laboratory tests. Providing veterinary care for each ailment that befalls your terrapin can quickly become an expensive affair.

To help protect you financially, countries like the United States and the United Kingdom offer health insurance policies for pets of many varieties, including exotic pet reptiles such as red-eared slider turtles. Healthcare and medical plans chalked up by these companies provide an umbrella of financial cover for such cases as shell-related ailments, respiratory, cardiac and intestinal diseases, rectal issues, vaccinations and even cancer.

In the United States, pet insurance policies are offered by such companies as Pet Assure and Nationwide Pet Insurance. In the United Kingdom, you can find pet insurance policies with companies like Exotic Direct and Cliverton.

Chapter 9: Breeding Red-eared Slider Turtles

1. Understanding the risks of Red-eared slider turtle breeding in captivity

If you have hatched a successful clutch of red-eared slider turtles in captivity, please take a moment to truly appreciate and celebrate your hard work. It is considered among the most challenging tasks to maintain the natural optimal nesting and incubation patterns in an artificial environment; that you have done so is a testament to your commitment. However, before you undertake this arduous task, it is wise to consider the amount of factors that surround the breeding and subsequent care for red-eared slider turtle hatchlings during each phase of the endeavor.

To begin with, breeding your red-eared slider turtles can be easily perfected with time and practice; this ease in routine could leave you with an uncontrollable rise in your personal hatchling population. Once hatched, the infants will require a specific environment within which to grow comfortably; any deviation or fluctuation from the accepted conditions could result in the death of the young ones.

Should you be able to successfully hatch the eggs, it then adds to your responsibility – and expenses – to provide a housing that allows them to develop through each stage of growth. This will include buying a number of tanks, changing the water constantly, doubling up on splitting feeding and cleaning duties between the adults and babies and installing new filtering, heating and lighting devices, to name a few. The hatchlings may also never be accepted by the adult community, than requiring you to maintain separate housing areas.

There is then the future problem of long-term care for the hatchlings. If successfully raised to their adult stage, you will have plenty of terrapins who survive and will need to be cared for till you can provide alternate housing for them. You can choose to sell them to interested individuals, or choose to sell them to a local reputed vendor, but these practices will have to be permitted and legal within your residence. Indeed, the entire process of breeding your adults or hatching the eggs, whether for personal use or profit, is futile without legal permits from the concerned authorities, and is definitely not permitted in such states as Florida.

Any feelings of dissatisfaction with the pet in terms of care, or feeling overwhelmed at the overall costs and work that goes into raising such a large group of red eared sliders may then prompt you or the new owners to either consider giving them up for adoption or releasing them into the wild. As members of the invasive species family, we now understand that this procedure may not only be traumatic for their welfare, but is also prohibited in several areas around the world. On a personal note, this endeavour, rewarding though it may be, will consume a large part of your free time, and require dedication, patience and support from the legal bodies at every stage. Each phase of the breeding process will also affect the people you live with, whether financially, emotionally and even physically, making it essential that they are cooperative of your plans. When you do decide to breed your red-eared slider turtles, take the time to consider the circumstances surrounding their breeding, and the number of factors you leave to chance – it will help you make a decision that works out for you.

2. Caring for the Eggs

Incubation and Hatching

Should you choose to have your red-eared slider eggs hatch, and have been permitted by the necessary Wildlife laws to do so, determine the process by which you'd like the hatchlings to emerge. If raised in the optimal housing conditions, your females, when ready, will lay up to 3 or 4 clutches of eggs in a single year. Do not be surprised if there is no male present at the time of egg-laying; females do not require mating rituals do lay eggs, simply to fertilize the eggs into developing embryos.

You can feel for these eggs in the female's rear region, between the carapace and hind legs, should she exhibit nesting behaviors or egg-binding symptoms. It may not be possible for your turtle to hatch all these eggs by herself successfully, especially in a captive environment. Working with your pet, you can provide the best incubation conditions - natural or artificial - to birth as many healthy hatchlings as possible.

Natural Incubation

The most obvious choice for incubation of your turtle eggs would be through the natural method - having the mother incubate and hatch the eggs herself. In the wild, a female red-eared slider turtle likes to dig up nesting spots deep into the soil to deposit her clutch of eggs for safe hatching. In captivity, she will look for similar nesting zones, signalling her readiness to lay eggs with frantic digging activity.

If you have provided a specific nesting zone for your pet, it is here that she will lay the eggs. An ideal nesting area would be at least 12 inches deep and contain a substrate made of organic compost soil and loamy sand in equal proportions. While looking for the perfect nest, the mothers prefer those spots that are free of such sharp objects and particles as gravel or stones. Ensure that your substrate is free of abrasive material to prevent egg binding, egg laying in water, or injury to your female.

Once the your female has laid her clutch, successful natural incubation should result in the eggs hatching between 60 to 80 days. In the event that your housing area is not suitable for natural incubation and hatching, you can provide the eggs with artificial incubation.

Artificial Incubation

Brooding is a process undertaken by the female turtle when she finishes depositing her clutch of eggs at her chosen nesting zone. If you collect the eggs in her absence at the end of each laying session, and repeatedly destroy unhatched eggs, her initial aggressive brooding instincts may diminish over time. When you collect the eggs with the purpose of hatching them, however, artificial incubation becomes essential.

Collecting turtle eggs requires slightly different handling than collecting poultry or fowl eggs would. From the moment they are laid, the eggs should be handled with utmost care, without being turned, shaken or placed in any other position. Those eggs that were laid in water and not collected immediately would have become non-viable, and are best disposed of.

The entire process of incubation takes up to 80 days, and you can find many commercially manufactured incubators that correctly serve this purpose. Incubating red-eared slider turtle eggs is a tricky procedure that requires specific temperature and humidity settings. Specifically-designed commercial incubators solve this problem by allowing you to regulate conditions with an inbuilt thermostat. For an economic option, a sturdy plastic container filled with vermiculite (to replicate natural nesting zone), drilled with strategically placed holes for ventilation will comfortably incubate your clutch.

The most interesting feature of artificial incubation is that it allows you to regulate the temperature of the nesting zone to determine what sex your hatchlings will be. Owing to the unique phenomena of gender determination via climatic temperatures, a temperature on the lower end of the accepted spectrum will give you male hatchlings, higher temperatures will hatch females, and a median transitory temperature may also result in transgender turtles!

3. Caring for the young
Even though you may undertake the incubation process with utmost care and caution, you still should not be disappointed if all the eggs don't hatch, or if they do, and the hatchlings do not survive. Red-eared slider turtle eggs, in captivity, have a slighter accelerated rate of hatching if undertaken carefully, but it is the complication in the subsequent care provided to the infant that raises their mortality rate as well.

Brooding zones for hatchlings are critical to their survival, whether they have hatched through the artificial or natural incubation method. You should shift the hatchlings into the infant housing set-up almost as soon as they hatch; this brooder can be a commercially manufactured predetermined one, or even a makeshift aquarium or container set up to house hatchlings.

Ensure that the brooding zone is housed away from direct light, heat, or wind. Adequate UVA and UVB lighting, along with a submersible water heater will also have to be fixed. A basking zone in a separate area should also be maintained for optimal growth; maintain the temperature of the water at 80 degrees Fahrenheit (26.6 degrees Celsius) and the basking areas at 90 degrees Fahrenheit (32.3 degrees Celsius). The water will also need to be supplemented with a filtration system, and cleaned out at least once a month.

While it is tricky to determine the exact moment of hatching, in an artificial setting, keeping a constant eye on the eggs between the 60th and 80th days will usually reward you with the sight of a hatchling red-eared slider turtle. Using a calcified tooth that protrudes from the tip of their mouth, the hatchlings chip away at the shell until they are free from its inner walls. They may, however, still be feeding off the contents of the yolk sac; if noticed on the hatchling plastron, allow the young one to dispose of the sac itself.

Newborn hatchlings survive best when fed with a specially-curated carnivorous starter diet, prepared to contain all the necessary nutrients, especially shell, bone and muscle building protein. The transition to a more herbivorous diet, such as vegetation and aquatic plants, is usually completed by the time the hatchling reaches a year in age. Some hatchlings may show an aversion to food at first, but can be enticed to feed and accept live feed and pellets.

During the first months of development, red-eared slider hatchlings are best left undisturbed; any excessive handling could cause injury or stress to the terrapin. As long as you make timely calm appearances to provide food and clean the tank, your hatchlings, in time, will grow to recognize you as their caregiver.

There is no hard evidence that advocates one method of hatching over the other. While the natural way seems like the best hatching technique, an artificial method of incubation may prove just as successful, provided these practices are permitted by the governing authorities in your area. The final choice to hatch red-eared slider turtles truly comes down your individual settings, preferences and expectations from your pets.

Chapter 10: The Essential Red-eared Slider Care Shopping List

The following list comprises all the items you will need to care for your red-eared slider turtle on a daily basis - from housing to diet, including accessories and healthcare items. Most of these products will be available at your local pet stores, whether in the United States, Canada or the United Kingdom.

Several companies also offer pet equipment and accessories for sale through online retail websites. In the United States and Canada, you can access Petco, PetSmart, Pet Mountain or That Pet Place to find items that address your pet care needs, while Exotic Pets, Online Reptile Shop, 888 Reptiles and Rainforest Supplies, offers the same services in the United Kingdom.

Housing

Glass tank, preferably with capacity between 40 and 125 gallons (for pair of red-eared sliders housed for breeding) or Plastic Storage Tub or Plastic Outdoor Storage Pool Cabinet, Brackets

Water Filters (such as Rena FilStar or AquaClear)

Water heaters - Submersible (100 or 200 watt, preferably 1 pair)

Basking platform (Zoo Med Turtle dock or Acrylic Turtle ramp)

Heating lamps (with ceramic/porcelain sockets, amount depending on the size of the tank and number of turtles)

Ceramic Heat Emitter (100 watt)

Fluorescent UVA/UVB bulbs (such as ReptiSun 10.0)

Pet-bedding (such as Burgess, ProRep or Pebbels and Gravel bags from Lowe's)

Electric timer

Large fish net

Wire/mesh screen

Water conditioning/testing kit

Diet

Fruits and Vegetables

Red lettuce leaf
Bananas
Bell pepper
Blackberries
Broccoli
Collard greens
Carrot tops
Cauliflower
Cherries
Chicory
Cranberries
Cucumber
Endives
Romaine lettuce leaves
Grapes
Honeydew melon
Kale

Apples
Mustard leaf
Nectarines
Oranges
Papaya
Turnip leaves
Peaches
Prickly Pears
Pineapple
Plums
Pomegranates
Raspberries
Green lettuce leaf
Sprouts
Strawberries
Watermelon
Mangoes

Flowers and plants

Duckweed
Water hyacinth
Water lettuce
Frog-bit
Anacharis
Pondweed
Water Starwort
Water Milofil

Nasturtium
Amazon Swords
Water Lily
Water Fern
Hornwort
Dandelion

Live feed

Earthworms
Super worms
Feeder fish
Guppies
Rosy-red minnows
Daphnia
Chicken
Turkey
Crickets
Shrimp (Gammarus)
Krill
Silkworms
Waxworms
Mosquito larvae
Pond snail
Tadpoles
Apple snail
Tubifex worms
Mealworms

Miscellaneous food items

Commercial-brand turtle pellets (FLuker's Aquatic Turtle Diet, Nasco Turtle Brittle, Tetra ReptoMin, Mazuri Freshwater Turtle Diet, etc.)
Boiled eggs
Brined shrimp/krill
Canned de-shelled snails

Healthcare

Cuttlefish bone
RepCal
Repti Turtle Sulfa Dip
Vitamin A Drops
Neosporin
Nolvasan
Betadine
Hibiclens
Baytril
Toothbrushes
Thermometers

Conclusion

Now that you are equipped with all the information that you need with respect to the red-eared slider turtle, I am sure that you will make a great owner. It takes a lot of work to keep this reptile at home. While that may sound intimidating, if you are unable to match all the requirements and needs of your pets, you will only compromise on their health and well-being. To conclude, I would like to remind you that raising a red-eared slider turtle is a big financial commitment.

Here is a breakdown of the approximate costs of keeping a red-eared slider turtle:

- Tank: $150 to $450 or £100 to £300

- Bedding: $6 to $30 or £4 to £20

- Feed: $4 to $10 or £3 to £7 for a 2 pound bag

- Water filters and testing kits: $60 to $175 or £40 to £120

- Heating: $30 to $65 or £20 to £40

- Lighting: $60 to $175 or £40 to £120

- Veterinary Care: $20 to $150 or £15 to £100

Once you are sure of making this commitment, you can convert your home into a great place for your red-eared slider turtle.

I hope this book answers all your questions about having red-eared slider turtle.

References

Seek to continually learn more about your red-eared slider turtle. As with the care of all exotic pets, new techniques, strategies and concepts in such areas as housing, diet, health care and breeding are discovered and implemented at a rapid rate. Never turn down an opportunity to learn more about your new pets, and eagerly seek out those who may know more than you do about these temperamental yet fascinating reptiles.

Books

Practical Encyclopedia of Keeping and Breeding Freshwater Turtles and Tortoises

By A.C. Highfield / Carapace Press 2006

Turtles of the United States and Canada

By Carl H. Ernst, Jeffrey E. Lovich and Roger W. Barbour / Smithsonian Institution Press, 1994

A Field Guide to Reptiles and Amphibians of Eastern and Central North America

Expanded by Roger Conant and Joseph T. Collins / Houghton Mifflin Company, 3rd Edition

Life History and Ecology of the Slider Turtle

BY Gibbons, J.W. / Smithsonian Institution Press, 1993

Keeping and Breeding Freshwater Turtles

By Ross Gurley / Living Art Publishing, 2003

Websites

Important Note: The websites mentioned in this book were active at the time of printing. However, by the time you read this book, the websites might no longer be active. That, of course, is out of my control as the Internet changes rapidly.

In the information age, learning more about your red-eared slider turtle is only a few clicks away. Be sure to bookmark these sites for quick access in the future.

Informational Websites

www.turtleforum.com

This website and message board contains plenty of information about red-eared slider turtle care and handling.

www.redearslider.com

The comprehensive care and education guide on the Red-eared slider turtle.

www.turtles.net

Turtles provides extensive knowledge on several types of chelonians, including the various breeds of red-eared slider turtle.

www.austinsturtlepage.com

A popular website with a thriving community forum featuring news, information and more concerning red-eared slider turtle and other common exotics.

www.allturtles.com

Information about most turtles native to North America. This site provides identification photos from most species and tips for spotting various species in the wild.

www.repticzone.com/

This website provides a variety of helpful resources, as well as information about red-eared slider care and purchase. You can also use this website to find information on breed standards, exotic pet fairs and meet other reptile enthusiasts.

www.turtletimes.com

Another popular website with a thriving community forum featuring news, information and more concerning red-eared slider turtle and other common exotics.

www.britishcheloniagroup.co.uk

This informative and well-maintained website has information on red-eared slider turtle, including data about wild colonies, behavioural patterns, etc.

Breeders

Red-eared slider turtle breeders are not only an excellent source for purchasing hatchlings; they can also provide a wealth of information through detailed and interactive forums posted on the Internet. At the time of writing, all the following links were active and functional; in the event that any source should re-direct you to an inactive page, please understand that the maintenance of these websites is subject to Internet-policies and the preferences of the website owners; we cannot claim personal responsibility for the same.

www.theturtlesource.com

THe Turtle Source sells hatchlings and eggs of red-eared slider turtle and many other poultry breeds.

www.backwaterreptiles.com

Backwater Reptiles houses a variety of chelonian species, and their website provides information about red-eared slider turtle housing, maintenance and feeding.

www.reptilecity.com

Reptile City is another go-to website for lesser-common exotic reptile species, and their website provides information about red-eared slider turtle housing, maintenance and feeding.

University and Governmental Resources

The US Geological Survey – Red-eared Slider Turtles

www.nas.er.usgs.gov

Although primarily focused on turkeys and chickens, this Oklahoma State University maintained website contains some information about red-eared slider turtle.

Massachusetts Legalities on Red-eared Slider Ownership

www.mass.gov

Maintained by the University of Michigan, the Animal Diversity Web has thousands of pages of information, detailing the lives of various animal species. In addition to reading about red-eared slider turtle, you can also learn about their predators, prey and competitors here.

Center for Integrated Agricultural Systems

www.californiaherps.com

This site, provided and maintained by the California Wildlife Authority, contains a wealth of data concerning all common local reptiles, including red-eared slider turtle.

The Centres for Disease Control and Prevention

www.cdc.gov

Based in Atlanta, Georgia, the CDC provides information on a variety of diseases that may be zoonotic. Additionally, the website provides further resources for coping with outbreaks of salmonella.

Veterinary Resources

Veterinarians.com

www.localvets.com/

This site is a search engine that can help you find a local veterinarian to treat your red-eared slider turtle.

Veterinary Care Specialists

www.vcsmilford.com

This website includes a veterinarian service as well as care-related information that may be useful for red-eared slider turtle Owners.

Holly House Vets

www.hollyhousevets.co.uk

A comprehensive website that covers various subjects like life history, care and breeding of different red-eared sliders, along with relevant veterinary resources in the UK.

Heartland Veterinary

www.heartlandveterinary.com

A comprehensive website that covers various subjects like life history, care and breeding of different red-eared sliders, along with relevant veterinary resources in the UK.

Avian Exotics

www.avianexoticsvet.com

Avian Exotics Vet provides care information as well as emergency and long-term medical services for red-eared slider turtles.

Published by IMB Publishing 2016

CPSIA information can be obtained
at www.ICGtesting.com
Printed in the USA
LVHW010316081118
596405LV00018B/581